MORE THAN
PETTICOATS

—⊰•⊱—

REMARKABLE
OREGON WOMEN

Gayle C. Shirley

TWODOT

For Steve

Cliché but so true, I couldn't have done it without you.

A · T W O D O T · B O O K

© 1998 Falcon® Publishing, Inc., Helena, Montana.

Printed in Canada.

2 3 4 5 6 7 8 9 0 TP 03 02 01 00

Visit our website at http://www.falconguide.com.

Design, typesetting, and other prepress work by Falcon® Publishing, Inc.

Cover photo taken on the Columbia River. Courtesy Oregon Historical Society—Or Hi 71994.

Library of Congress Cataloging-in-Publication Data

Shirley, Gayle Corbett.
    More than petticoats : remarkable Oregon women / Gayle C. Shirley.
        p.   cm.
    Includes bibliographical references (p. 128–134) and index.
    Contents: Marie Dorion -- Anna Maria Pittman Lee -- Tabitha
Moffatt Brown -- Abigail Scott Dunway -- Bethenia Owens-Adair --
Mary Leonard -- Lola Greene Baldwin -- Alice Day Pratt -- Hazel Hall
-- Opal Whiteley.
    ISBN 1-56044-668-4   (pbk. : alk. paper)
    1. Women--Oregon--Biography. 2. Oregon--Biography. I. Title.
CT3260.S455   1998
920.72'09795--dc21   98-45293
                                                                 CIP

When the true history of woman's agency in up-building the State of Oregon shall have been written, the world will marvel at the sublimity of the inspiration of the man, or men, who gave to the seal of the state its enduring motto, *alis volat propriis*, or "she flies with her own wings."

Abigail Scott Duniway

$\mathscr{C}$ONTENTS

${\mathscr{A}}$CKNOWLEDGMENTS

${\mathscr{T}}$hank goodness for libraries and the patient people who staff them. I could never have produced this book without the help of research librarians and photo researchers at the Multnomah County Library and the Oregon Historical Society in Portland; the Harvey W. Scott Memorial Library at Pacific University in Forest Grove, Oregon; the Crook County Library in Prineville, Oregon; the Lewis and Clark County Library in Helena, Montana; and the Great Falls Public Library in Great Falls, Montana— not to mention the many libraries that responded to my hefty stacks of interlibrary loan requests.

I owe an especially large debt of gratitude to Sieglinde Smith, research librarian at the Oregon Historical Society, who reviewed the manuscript and made valuable suggestions. Any factual errors that remain in the book are my fault, not hers. Cecil Housel, a photo researcher at Oregon Historical Society, tracked down many of the photos that enliven the book.

In addition, I want to thank for their assistance David Milholland, president of the Oregon Cultural Heritage Commission in Portland; Carolyn James, archivist with the Oregon Department of Transportation in Salem; Steve Sechrist, director of public affairs at Pacific University; Gordon Gillespie, director of the Bowman Museum in Prineville; and Fred W. Decker, of Corvallis.

Of course, thanks to my editor, Megan Hiller, who was patient and understanding when times got tough.

INTRODUCTION

There is an axiom that women *are* history but men *make* history. That certainly has been the case for all too many generations. For two centuries after our forefathers gave birth to our nation, presumably without the help of foremothers, every American student studied a history made up of kings, presidents, emperors, and generals. History books were laden with patrilineal family trees, etchings of famous male warriors and leaders, and maps of battlefields where men slaughtered other men as they conquered new lands.

But in the 1960s and 1970s, women did make history. In the course of what became known as the feminist revolution, they demanded recognition of their value and contributions—today, tomorrow, and yesterday. In the two decades since, historians have begun taking a serious look at the role women played in the building of our nation. Eventually they trained their spotlights on women of the West—those who came by steamboat, train, and covered wagon, and those who already were here.

At first, scholars shuffled Western women into convenient pigeonholes. There was the idealized "madonna of the prairies," a long-suffering pioneer wife and mother who gamely toiled across the Great Plains in calico and sunbonnet. There was the disreputable "soiled dove," an enterprising floozy who made her living in hurdy-gurdys and houses of ill repute. There were the maiden schoolmarms, the servile "squaws," and the pistol-packing Calamity Janes.

But as historians unearthed letters and diaries left behind by flesh-and-blood frontier women, and as they learned more about the Native American and Hispanic women who were here before, they discovered there were no convenient stereotypes. The women of the Old West were as diverse as the Oregon landscape. They came from different backgrounds, had different experiences, and responded to frontier life in different ways.

For some, the move west was like taking off a corset—very liberating. The frontier offered new opportunities to express their individuality. For others, the West was a land of privation and hardship where the struggle to survive overrode other desires. For others, the West was simply an extension of the East. They brought with them all the repressive baggage of the "cult of true womanhood," which demanded that they be pious, pure, submissive, and domestic.

"If there is one truth about frontierswomen," Glenda Riley, author of *Women on the American Frontier*, contends, "It is that they were not any one thing."

This wealth of diversity is apparent in the following pages, which celebrate ten remarkable women who made their mark on Oregon history.

One hazard inherent in writing about the past is the tendency to view historical events from a contemporary perspective. Yet, how can we do otherwise? We're all products of our times. Values and attitudes change, and what may have been socially acceptable a century ago may not be "politically correct" now. This is especially apparent with regard to women and minorities.

I've tried to keep modern sensibilities in mind as I've written this book—but not at the expense of historical accuracy. For how can we judge how far we've come if we refuse to acknowledge where we've been? The fact is, women and minorities were considered inferior a century ago, and that attitude is apparent in some of the quotations I've used in this book. That we know better today doesn't mean it's our job to erase incidents of sexism and racism from our history books and pretend they never existed. Our responsibility, I believe, is to recognize them for what they were and demonstrate with our own behavior that civilization has made progress.

When I began work on this book, my first challenge was to identify ten or so women who were worthy of inclusion. At first, I feared I would never find enough, but as I dug into historical archives, I developed a new worry: How was I to decide which of countless fascinating women to include? How could I be sure I wouldn't overlook someone important?

To keep the book a manageable length, I chose to limit it to women born before 1900. In some cases I was forced to leave out women who deserve mention but who are not discussed much in historical records. For example, Polly Holmes, a slave who came to Oregon with her master in 1844, was involved in the state's most famous emancipation case. Her husband, Robbin, sued to regain custody of their three children from their ex-master, a man named Nathaniel Ford. The couple persevered and won the landmark case, but historical records reveal little about Polly Holmes's involvement.

I also have left out prominent women who played a role in the history of parts of the Oregon Territory that now lie outside the state boundaries. For example, you won't find chapters in this book on architect-nun Mother Joseph or missionary Narcissa Whitman, but you can find their compelling stories in *More than Petticoats: Remarkable Washington Women.*

Finally, I chose a cross-section of women who excelled in various fields—from doctor, lawyer, and university founder to enterpreneur and author.

I'm sure readers will be able to think of other women who deserve to be featured in this book but aren't. I regret leaving out any of those women. The fact is, all of the women who helped to shape Oregon were remarkable—those who tirelessly pounded animal hides into supple leather to clothe their families; those who waited out blizzards in homesteader shacks; those who packed lunch pails for husbands headed to the wharves and sawmills; and those who raised money to build churches, schools, and libraries.

They were all heroines. They all helped make Oregon what it is today.

MARIE DORION
1785–1850

Madonna of the Oregon Trail

On a January evening in 1814, Marie Dorion was preparing dinner at a Pacific Fur Company post when a friend arrived with alarming news: A band of Bannock Indians had plundered a nearby fur-trapping camp and was headed for the camp of Marie's husband, Pierre, and his three partners.

Marie, who was herself half Indian, decided that she had to warn the men. She bundled up her young sons, Jean Baptiste and Paul, slung them onto a horse, and plodded through rain and mud for three days to reach Pierre's camp. As she approached it, she met one of her husband's comrades, a man named LeClerc. He was badly wounded and weak from loss of blood. As he struggled to stay on his feet, he haltingly told Marie that Indians had robbed and murdered Pierre and the other two trappers that morning. Marie had arrived several hours too late.

Suddenly, a rustling in some nearby brush startled Marie. Had the killers returned? Would they attack her and her sons?

She was relieved to discover that the sound had been made by some horses left behind by the marauders. A large, strong woman, she captured two of the animals and hoisted LeClerc onto one and

This historical signpost was erected in northeastern Oregon near the spot where Marie Dorion gave birth to her third son.

her sons onto the other. Then she, too, mounted, and they headed back toward the main trapping camp near what is now Caldwell, Idaho.

As they slogged along, LeClerc grew faint from loss of blood and tumbled from his horse. Fearful that the Bannocks would discover them, Marie hid him and her boys in the brush. She tried to tend the trapper's wounds, but they were too serious. LeClerc died during the night. The next morning, Marie covered his body with branches and snow and set out with her boys for the main camp once again.

Marie desperately hoped to find refuge at the post, but what she found instead was horrific. During her absence, the trappers there had been murdered and scalped and their bodies mutilated. Frantically, Marie collected some food, loaded it onto a pair of horses, and fled toward what is now Oregon.

Wolves howled in the distance and snow obscured the trail as Marie and her sons rode westward. Soon they faced another obstacle, the Snake River. They forded it and reached the other side drenched but alive.

When they got to the Blue Mountains in northeastern Oregon, Marie faced yet another dilemma. One of the horses had collapsed. Should she press on with the one faltering animal she had left, or should she make camp and wait for the harsh weather to pass?

Marie decided to wait. She slaughtered the horses and smoked the meat. Then she built a hut of cedar branches, grass, and the horses' hides. For the next two months, mother and sons lived on horse meat, frozen berries, the inner bark from trees, and occasional mice and squirrels Marie caught in snares made of horsehair.

In late March, a warm spring breeze began to melt the snow, so the Dorions resumed their trek. But Nature proved fickle. On their second day out, a blizzard struck, and the intensely white snowscape temporarily blinded Marie. The family camped for three more days until her vision improved.

Marie and her sons reached the plains fifteen days after abandoning their winter camp. Their food was gone, but a pillar of smoke on the horizon gave them hope. Uncertain whether the fire marked a friendly camp or a hostile one, Marie hid her boys beneath a rock outcropping and, too exhausted to walk, crawled toward the encampment on the Columbia River. She was relieved to find a village of friendly Walla Wallas, who welcomed her and sent a search party to retrieve her boys.

While Marie and her sons recuperated, someone spotted a group of trappers paddling up the Columbia. The Pacific Fur Company had sent a search party to look for the company's employees in Idaho. From Marie, they learned that they would find none of them alive. Author Jerome Peltier described their reaction to her tale:

> Her listeners were horrified to learn that all of the party except herself, Baptiste, and Paul, had been so cruelly slaughtered. They were duly amazed by the fact that she and her children had survived. No doubt she was the subject of many tales told around the camp fires thereafter.

Campfire tales are notorious for inflating over time, and assorted written accounts of Marie's journey differ in some respects. But the basic elements of all of them are the same: After Marie's husband and the other trappers were murdered, Marie made an extraordinary wintertime flight through the mountains to save herself and her sons.

Remarkable as Marie's dramatic odyssey was, it was not the only chapter of her life to kindle a compelling campfire tale. Two years earlier, in 1811 and 1812, Marie had made history when she traveled with the Overland Astorians from St. Louis, Missouri, to what would become Astoria, Oregon.

Marie was the only woman in this party of trappers whom New York fur dealer John Jacob Astor had sent to the Pacific Northwest in the hope of establishing a fur-trading empire. Though she got pregnant during the trip, she walked much of the way, shepherding her two young sons through rugged, unfamiliar country. Near the end of the eleven-month journey, Marie gave birth to the first known child with any white blood to be born in the Oregon country. The baby didn't survive, but Marie and her family did reach the mouth of the Columbia River, where the trappers built a trading post they called Astoria. She was the first woman and mother to travel the route that would become the Oregon Trail, a feat that earned her the title "Madonna of the Oregon Trail."

It also inspired historians and writers to immortalize her. "Name, if you can, any female character in history whose story outshines in pluck, grim determination, fierce resolution, and mother self-sacrifice the record of this red heroine in letters of blood," author Byron Defenbach wrote in the florid prose of the early twentieth century.

Marie's feats are notable by any standard, but she has been overshadowed in history books by another Indian woman, Sacagawea. The two were contemporaries: Both were born in the 1780s, and both lived in St. Louis in about 1810. However, there are no records indicating that they ever met.

Marie, who was half Iowa Indian and half French Canadian, became the property and common-law wife of Pierre Dorion in 1804. He, too, was of mixed blood. His mother was a Sioux Indian and his father a French Canadian who traveled with the Lewis and Clark expedition. Pierre and Marie first settled near what is now Yankton, South Dakota. Their first son, Jean Baptiste, was born in 1806, and Paul followed a few years later. The family moved to St. Louis in 1810.

Wilson Price Hunt, of the Pacific Fur Company, was head-quartered in St. Louis about that time, recruiting sixty men for an expedition to Oregon. Hunt wanted to enlist Pierre because of his knowledge of the country and tribes along the Missouri River. Dorion also spoke several Indian languages, and he was a good hunter and guide as well. Hunt offered Pierre three hundred dollars a year—a better-than-average wage in those days.

However, Pierre was far from an ideal employee. He liked to drink, and when he did he grew mean as a wolverine. Even when he wasn't drunk, Pierre was obstinate. At the last minute, he refused to join Hunt's expedition unless his wife and sons could accompany him. Hunt had reservations about taking a woman and two young children along, but he eventually relented. He needed Pierre's services too badly to refuse.

Occasionally Marie must have regretted joining the expedition. Soon after the group left St. Louis, she and Pierre had some heated arguments. Twice, Pierre got drunk and throttled her. Once, Marie ran off with her sons and hid along the river. She agreed to rejoin the party only after Pierre was sober. Pierre's rampages eventually ended, probably because he had no access to liquor in the wilderness.

Marie's hardships did not end. In Wyoming, the trappers toiled across badlands and buttes, rivers and ridges. They went hungry when game grew scarce. Marie had the added responsibility of keeping track of her children, who were now about five and two years old. "To observers she showed no sign of breaking under these difficult conditions and withstood the rigor of the trail as well as any of the men," author Peltier noted.

When the travelers reached the Snake River, they cached most of their supplies and fashioned fifteen rickety dugouts from cotton-wood trees lining the banks. They hoped to save time and energy by floating through Idaho, but they were no match for the raging river.

Several boats overturned and spilled their cargo into the rapids. Two men were tossed from their boats and drowned. The survivors finally abandoned the dugouts. From then on they referred to the Snake as that "accursed mad river."

Walking was not much easier. The group slowly picked its way over rocky ridges, sloshed through mountain streams, and maneuvered around deep chasms. Game grew scarce again, and the expedition members slaughtered some of their horses to avoid starvation. They also traded with Indians for scraps of salmon and dog and horse meat.

To the relief of Marie, who was nearing the end of her third pregnancy, Pierre traded a buffalo robe for a horse so that she could ride and rest her weary body. When Hunt wanted to butcher the animal to feed his men, Pierre refused to let him, despite Hunt's bribes and threats. Most of the other men gallantly concurred with Pierre's decision in spite of their gnawing hunger.

In late December 1811, the party forded the icy Powder River twice and marched through the Grande Ronde Valley. They paused for the night near what is now North Powder, Oregon. Washington Irving described what happened next in his classic 1836 account of the trip, *Astoria:*

> Early the following morning the squaw of Pierre Dorion, who had hitherto kept on without murmuring or flinching, was suddenly taken in labor, and enriched her husband with another child. As the fortitude and good conduct of the poor woman had gained for her the good-will of the party, her situation caused concern and perplexity. Pierre, however, treated the matter as an occurrence that could be arranged and need cause no delay. He remained by his wife in the camp, with his other

children and his horse, and promised soon to rejoin the main body, who proceeded on their march.

The Astorians struggled to an Indian village near present-day La Grande, Oregon, where they feasted on dog and horse meat and roots. The next day, Pierre and Marie and their three children rejoined them. Marie had jounced twenty miles on horseback only a day after giving birth, but as she rode into camp carrying her newborn infant and two-year-old son, she "looked as unconcerned as if nothing had happened to her," according to Irving.

The baby did not fare as well. It died on January 7. Pierre whispered a short prayer, and the family buried it in an unmarked grave. Ironically, the gravesite was not far from where Marie would hide her two children while she crawled for help two years later. Today, a historical signpost marks the spot near North Powder.

Oregonians have honored Marie in other ways. Her name was inscribed on a plaque in the capitol in Salem. A dormitory at Eastern Oregon University in La Grande bears her name.

After Marie's daring flight to safety in 1814, she continued to live in the Pacific Northwest. In 1818, she married Louis Joseph Venier, and the couple had a daughter named Marguerite. After Venier was killed by Indians, Marie married a third time, probably in 1824. Her new husband, Jean Baptiste Toupin, was an interpreter for the Hudson's Bay Company at Fort Nez Perce, which was later renamed Fort Walla Walla. The couple moved to the Willamette Valley in the early 1840s, and there, at the St. Louis Catholic Church, Marie was baptized and her marriage to Toupin legitimized on July 19, 1841. The priest told the couple that the ceremony also would legitimize their two children, Francis and Marie Anne, as well as Marie's children from her earlier marriages, Marguerite and Jean Baptiste. When the priest asked whether Marie had other children, she realized that she had forgotten to mention Paul, her second-born son. She seldom thought of him because he had run off to live with Indians as a boy. Marie had no idea what had become of him.

But a few historians have traced Paul. He is listed as "Paul Dorio" on the books of the Rocky Mountain Fur Company as early as 1827, when he would have been about eighteen. Francis Parkman, in his book *The Oregon Trail*, told how he met Paul in 1846 at Fort Laramie, Wyoming. Parkman described him as "a shriveled little figure" with "keen snakelike eyes," a face like an "old piece of leather," and a mouth that "spread from ear to ear."

Paul's older brother, Jean Baptiste, became a guide and interpreter and served as a lieutenant in the Oregon Rifle Company during the Cayuse War of 1847–1850.

Marie lived the rest of her life at French Prairie near present-day Salem. Dr. Elijah White, an early Oregon pioneer, met her and was "very much impressed with her noble, commanding, bearing." She presented the doctor with several pairs of handmade moccasins.

Marie died on September 5, 1850, and was buried "under the steeple" of the St. Louis Catholic Church. She was granted this special honor, according to historian T. C. Elliott, because she was "looked up to and revered as an extraordinary woman, the oldest in the neighborhood, kindly, patient and devout. This must have been so, else burial under special dispensation 'in the church' instead of in the nearby cemetery would not have been possible."

The prominent role Marie played in Oregon history is also reflected in the fact that she was generally addressed as "Madame." How she got the title is unclear. Early French Canadian settlers of the Willamette Valley reportedly called her "Madame Iowa" after her tribe of origin. The title was first used in print by author Frances Fuller Victor, in the 1870 edition of her book *River of the West*.

Historian Peltier believed that Marie earned the honorific because of her "native, inherent qualities" and her special place in American history. According to him,

> Marie Iowa is the only known Indian lady who was given the title "Madame" by her white neighbors and historians. With certainty she must have deserved it. ... Various family traditions and local histories tell us she was honored and revered. ❖

Anna Maria Pittman Lee

1803–1838

Missionary Bride

𝒯he missionaries gathered in a grove suffused with the fragrance of firs, the chirrup of birds, and the warmth of the summer sun. On this fine day—July 16, 1837—the men and women had come to this spot beside the Willamette River to celebrate the first communion in Oregon. They were joined by several Indians decked in beads and feathers, a handful of French Canadians and their Indian wives, and a cluster of Indian children who lived at the mission house nearby.

The Reverend Jason Lee, the mission superintendent, opened the ceremony with a hymn and a prayer. Then, to the surprise of the congregation, the gangly minister left the pulpit to take the arm of Anna Maria Pittman, a tall, dark-haired teacher who had recently joined the mission. The couple returned to the primitive altar and were married by Jason's nephew, the Reverend Daniel Lee.

Anna Maria had known her new husband a mere two months, but that had been long enough to see that he was a pious Christian and a dedicated missionary. That, in her mind, was significant, because she, too, longed to spread the gospel in the wilderness.

The bond between Anna Maria and Jason grew quickly, nur-

Anna Maria Pittman Lee

tured by their mutual devotion to God, the demanding work of the mission, and the happy news that they would soon be parents. But it was not long before the bond was tested. Only eight months after their wedding, Jason decided to leave on an eighteen-month trip to the East Coast to recruit volunteers and funding for his cause.

"If we never meet again on earth, how pleasing it will be, even in eternity, to reflect on the pleasant life we have led since we became one," Anna Maria wrote to her husband shortly after he left Oregon.

The letter was prophetic. Almost three months later, Anna Maria died giving birth to a son in a darkened room at the log mission. The newborn child did not survive.

Although Anna Maria lived in Oregon for only thirteen months, she nevertheless left her mark on the history of the region. She would be remembered as the first white woman to be married in Oregon, the first to give birth, die, and be buried there. She helped pave the way for Oregon's first wave of settlers by demonstrating that optimism, grace, and devotion to God were good antidotes to the rigors and loneliness of the frontier.

Anna Maria had come a long way, both physically and culturally, from the world she knew while growing up in New York City. She was born on September 24, 1803, the first of thirteen children of George and Mary Pittman. As was customary for the times, she had to help raise her younger siblings, so she had little opportunity to cultivate prospects for marriage.

She did manage to find time for worship and fellowship at the Allen Street Methodist Church, where she was enthralled by descriptions of the church's missionary work. At one missionary society meeting, she listened to two young preachers, Jason and Daniel Lee, outline their plans to head west to convert the Indians.

Their intentions reminded her of the tales of John Jacob Astor, a friend and business associate of her father who had established a short-lived fur-trading company in the Pacific Northwest. As a child, she had listened as Astor extolled the Oregon country. Now, as an adult, she again felt the pull of the West.

The leaders of the Methodist Missionary Society were reluctant to exploit her zeal, but they changed their minds in 1835 after Jason Lee pleaded for more help at his Oregon mission. Anna Maria was still begging them to send her to Oregon, so they agreed to pay her three hundred dollars to teach children at the mission. One of the church leaders suggested another, more intimate, assignment: Perhaps Anna Maria should marry Jason Lee.

Anna Maria was thoroughly disconcerted. Now thirty-two years old, she had long ago abandoned the idea of marriage. She explained that she wasn't interested in matrimony; she was eager to minister to the "poor dying red men." She refused to discuss the matter of marriage further.

In July 1836, Anna Maria and twelve other prospective missionaries boarded the ship *Hamilton* for the voyage of almost twenty thousand miles around Cape Horn to Oregon. She passed the months at sea by reading, knitting, sewing, singing, jumping rope, and writing letters home.

"Thirty-three years of my life forever gone, and alas how little of that time has been spent in doing good," she wrote to her parents on her birthday. "Oh if my life is spared another year I trust I shall be enabled to do something for God, who has done so much for me."

The *Hamilton* dropped anchor on December 23 at what is now Honolulu, Hawaii. Since the ship was not going any farther, the passengers had to wait several months for another ship bound for Oregon. Anna Maria never complained about the extended stay—after all, the tropical paradise was a pleasant diversion—but she was shocked by some of the islanders' behavior.

"This [is a] delightful place it exceeds my expectations," she exclaimed in a letter to her family. "Every house has a large garden and door yard full of trees full of shrub[b]ery. . . . This is a great place for musquetoes. We all sleep under nets. . . . There are many temptations here for white men who are not Christians. [T]heir examples have a very bad influence on natives."

After three months on the island, Anna Maria was eager to sail. "Time is flying, the heathen are dying without God; oh how much there is to be done, and short the time to do it in," she wrote in another letter to her family.

The missionaries boarded the *Diana* in April. Three severe gales battered the ship during a "boisterous" month at sea, but it reached the Oregon Territory safely and docked at Fort Vancouver on May 17, 1837. The little band was met by Dr. John McLoughlin, chief agent for the Hudson's Bay Company, who assured the group that Lee was on his way to escort them to the mission. When Lee arrived, McLoughlin introduced the reinforcements one by one. Anna Maria stood shyly off to one side. The teasing remarks and mischievous glances of her fellow travelers were making her uncomfortable. She was the last person McLoughlin introduced to the man she had been asked to marry.

According to an account written in 1848 by A. J. Allen, as Lee took her hand, "a light blush rose to her cheek, and a slight trepidation, which added to the charm of her manner, was all the evidence that she was conscious to any peculiarity in her position. . . . That Mr. Lee was pleased could be easily discovered from the complaisance of his bearing and the trouble he took to render himself agreeable."

The missionaries spent several days preparing for their trip up the Willamette River in a small boat and three canoes. On their day of departure, they scrambled into the boats so quickly that Anna Maria and Jason Lee were forced to take the last canoe together.

Anna Maria was relieved that Jason didn't mention marriage as their Indian crew paddled them upstream. Instead, the pair talked optimistically of the land and their hopes for converting the natives. Anna Maria soon got a taste of the task ahead when the group floated past an Indian village.

"I was the first white lady ever witnessed [by] them," she wrote in a letter to her parents. "[H]ere was an Indian village, a poor degraded set of beings inhabit it almost naked."

It took the emigrants two days to reach the mission about sixty miles south of the mouth of the Willamette River. When they spotted it, they realized that their lives were about to change dramatically, as author Theressa Gay noted in her book *The Life and Letters of Mrs. Jason Lee:*

What a contrast it was to the homes they had left some ten months before. Here they found a rough log house of two rooms, a kitchen and a school room, all quite devoid of the many comforts to which they had been accustomed. Here lived thirty Indian children under the care of the mission. Seven of them then lay ill, some of them dangerously, with no other bed than a mat and some blankets on the floor. The others, somewhat unkempt, gazed at the new arrivals with considerable curiosity.

The newcomers could see that there was plenty of work to do, and they immediately pitched in to build an addition to the log mission house. Anna Maria was assigned the time-consuming tasks of making meals and supervising the children. Yet she still found time to get better acquainted with Jason by riding horseback with him to nearby Indian villages. Some of the other missionaries wondered if the couple discussed marriage on these private excursions. When they asked the minister of his intentions, he replied, "Though a lady should travel the world over in order to become my wife, yet I could never consent to marry her, unless upon acquaintance I should become satisfied, that the step would be conducive to our mutual happiness and the glory of God."

Jason confessed in his diary that he had not fancied Anna Maria when they had met for the first time in New York, but in Oregon Jason overcame his misgivings. He was impressed by Anna Maria's hard work, her solicitous care of the children, and her devotion to the missionary cause. Within two weeks of her arrival, he asked for her hand in marriage.

Anna Maria didn't respond immediately. She needed time to pray and think. She barely knew this tall, slightly stooped man, but she saw that he was compassionate and devout. She decided to accept, as she confided in a letter to her parents: "I expect to give my heart and hand to J. Lee. [W]hen this union will take place I am not prepared to say. [B]ut probably soon."

Her mind made up, Anna Maria wasn't sure how to inform Lee of her decision. She enjoyed writing poetry, so she decided to communicate her acceptance in verse:

> Yes, where thou goest I will go,
> With thine my earthly lot be cast;
> In pain or pleasure, joy or woe,
> Will I attend thee to the last.

Anna Maria and Jason Lee told no one of their engagement. They decided simply to come forward and take their wedding vows during the first communion service. Two other couples already planned to marry that day. Author Gay described the ceremony:

On this historic day, God's sanctuary was a beautiful grove

of fir trees, which was located about forty rods east of the Mission House. At eleven o'clock the entire group of missionaries and their assistants, together with the twenty or thirty Indian and half-breed children under their care, went to this outdoor temple. Here they found assembled nearly all the inhabitants of the neighboring settlement, many of whom, no doubt, had been attracted by the news that a wedding was to take place. . . .

A more picturesque setting could not have been found for the ceremonies which were to be solemnized. Nearby rippled the limpid waters of the beautiful Willamette River. The stately firs, their giant branches silhouetted against the azure sky, formed a perfect backdrop. A pine fragrance, like that of incense, filled the air. At the same time the trees sang a calm refrain as the breeze gently rustled through the boughs. All nature seemed to be attuned to this eventful occasion.

After opening the service, Jason announced that he was ready to "practice what I have so often recommended" about the importance of marriage. He led Anna Maria to the altar, where they were married by Daniel Lee. Later, Jason returned to the pulpit to marry the two other couples.

Jason and Anna Maria had to postpone their honeymoon because of pressing mission projects, but a month later the pair joined Cyrus and Susan Shepard, one of the other couples married the same day, on a week-long horseback trip to the Pacific Coast. They waded in the surf, feasted on fish and clams, and camped beneath the pine and cedar trees.

After returning to the mission, located about ten miles northwest of present-day Salem, Anna Maria busied herself with household chores. She sewed clothes, baked pies and bread, churned twelve pounds of butter a week, and taught Sunday school classes. She thrived on her work—and her married life. She wrote to her brother George, who lived in the East, "I hope you are as happy with your wife as I am with my husband." In another letter she confided that she once sang of "the blessings of Celibacy" but now rejoiced in the "happiness of Matrimony!"

While Anna Maria's letters and poems from these days rang with expressions of joy, they also acknowledged that death could strike at any time—not an unrealistic expectation on the wild frontier. In a letter to her mother, she announced that by the time the letter arrived "if my life is spared I shall have become a mother."

Just as she had feared, Anna Maria's health and happiness would soon be tested. The leaders of the fledgling mission realized they needed help in order to spread the gospel to more Indian tribes. Jason agreed to make the long overland trip to the East to recruit more missionaries and solicit financial support. He expected to be gone for a year and a half.

His departure on March 26, 1838, was particularly painful because Anna Maria was six months pregnant. He knew he would miss the birth of his child. Anna Maria and Jason said their good-byes on the riverbank; then Anna Maria went home and collapsed on her bed. Half an hour later she was back on her feet, preparing a meal.

Anna Maria remained stoic. She understood how important God's work was to her husband. "I did not marry you to hinder, but rather to aid you in the performance of your duty," she wrote in a letter to him.

Still, the separation was a great strain for Anna Maria, as she endured a difficult pregnancy. She often felt sick and had to rest in bed. She sought solace in her strong faith in God, praying, singing hymns, and reading her Bible.

Another missionary, Elvira Perkins, claimed she had never seen

ANNA MARIA PITTMAN LEE

Anna Maria in "so happy a state of mind" as she was toward the end of her pregnancy. "She seemed perfectly resigned to the will of God, and ripening for heaven," Perkins said.

When her time finally came, Anna Maria's labor pains were excruciating, and the mission physician was alarmed. He had to use all the tools at his disposal to deliver the baby boy, who struggled and died two days later. Anna Maria faltered, too. Shortly before sunrise on June 26, 1838, she opened her eyes long enough to murmur, "I am going to my rest." As the sun's first rays gilded the hills, Anna Maria died.

The thirty-five-year-old mother and her infant son were laid together in a wooden casket fashioned by the mission carpenter and buried in the same grove in which Anna Maria had so recently been married. Years later, their remains were moved to the missionary plot in the Lee Mission Cemetery at Salem.

Two months after Anna Maria's death, a messenger caught up with Jason at Westport, Missouri, and delivered the tragic news. Lee later wrote that he "was awaked from a sweet slumber to receive the sad intelligence, and know and feel, more sensibly than it is in the power of human language to portray, that I was a lonely widower and a bereaved father. . . . [N]ever did I more sensibly feel my need of divine aid than in that trying hour."

Jason stifled his sorrow and continued his trip. With the help of two Indian boys who traveled with him, he raised thousands of dollars for his mission. At one stop, church members contributed thirty dollars for the education of an Indian girl who would be named Anna Maria Pittman.

At another stop in Vermont, Jason was introduced to Lucy Thomson, a twenty-eight-year-old seminary student who was deeply interested in missionary work. Jason was equally interested in Lucy. He extended his stay, wooed her, and then asked for her hand in marriage. She accepted and, after the marriage ceremony, they sailed for Oregon. Accompanying them were forty-eight men, women, and children who would reinforce the mission.

Jason brought with him a white-marble tombstone for the grave of his son and first wife. Carved on its face was this passage from the Book of Matthew:

Lo! we have left all
and
followed thee
What shall we have therefore?

The epitaph, as well as Anna Maria's letters and poems, reflect a devotion to God as strong as the current of the Columbia. Her faith helped her cope with isolation, hardship, and physical pain. It also bolstered her brief but loving relationship with her husband, who would long be remembered as one of the founding fathers of Oregon. One of the last letters that Anna Maria wrote to him proclaimed her love—and reminded him that they would see each other again, on earth or in heaven:

As I retired on [M]onday night I thought, [h]usband is not here to lie down with me. [B]ut it immediately occurred to me, God is here, and if I have his presence, and protection it will be well with me. If our lives are spared, how happy shall we be to embrace each other on your return; but if it is otherwise determined by our heavenly Father, I trust our ransomed spirits shall meet in that better world.... In the closest union and bonds of love. I remain your affectionate wife untile [sic] death. ✤

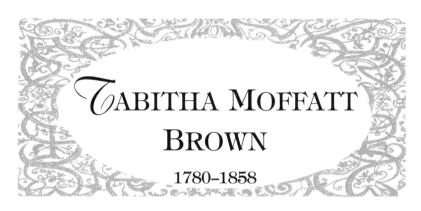

TABITHA MOFFATT BROWN

1780–1858

Mother of Oregon

*T*abitha Moffatt Brown, an elderly widow who weighed less than a hundred pounds, guided her horse through the rugged Umpqua Mountains of southern Oregon. Beside her on that frigid fall day in 1846 rode her brother-in-law, John Brown, a seventy-seven-year-old retired sea captain.

The two weary travelers were part of a wagon train that had left Missouri for the Oregon Territory seven months earlier. They had ridden ahead of the others because the emigrants' food supply was almost gone and word had passed among the wagons to "fly, everyone who can, from starvation." That morning, before leaving her daughter and son-in-law, who had to remain behind to round up the family's few livestock, Tabitha had eaten only three slices of bacon and sipped a cup of tea. She hoped to overtake another wagon train that had passed them the previous day and ask its members to share a bit of food.

Tabitha was traveling with a light load. Like many other settlers who had made the grueling trek to Oregon, she had watched her wagon splinter to pieces as it jolted over the rocky trail. She had been forced to abandon many precious belongings.

Tabitha Moffatt Brown

Now she faced another crisis. Captain Brown was complaining of a "swimming in his head and a pain in his stomach." As they picked their way through the trees and boulders, he toppled from his horse and lay on the ground, too feeble to climb back into the saddle.

Heavy rain clouds crept among the peaks, and Tabitha realized she had little time to act before a storm broke. She dared not dismount, because she didn't know if she could get back on her horse. So she held out a cane to the delirious old man so he could haul himself to his feet. She found a low spot where his horse could stand as she pulled him onto its back. Then, leading his horse by its reins, she searched for a campsite where she could put up a tent, cover her brother-in-law with blankets, and do her best to keep him warm through the night. She doubted he would survive until morning. Years later, she described her grim predicament:

> Pause for a moment and consider the situation. Worse than alone, in a savage wilderness, without food, without fire, cold and shivering, wolves fighting and howling all around me. Dark clouds hid the stars. All as solitary as death. But that same kind Providence that I had always known was watching over me still. I committed all to Him and felt no fear.

To Tabitha's great relief, Captain Brown rallied. The next morning, as she saddled their horses and prepared to break camp, a settler out deer hunting stumbled upon them. He shared some venison and helped them find their way back to the trail. They forged on to their destination: the lush Willamette Valley.

Tabitha had traveled close to two thousand miles through deserts, mountains, and valleys—often, she later recalled, with "mud, rocks, and water up to our horses' sides." She had feared attack by wild animals and hostile Indians. On some days, she had gone hungry. When at last she reached Oregon, she was practically penniless, but the sixty-six-year-old pioneer had clearly proven her mettle.

Tabitha's odyssey was remarkable, but she had yet to create her most lasting legacy. During her cross-country journey, she had witnessed the suffering of children whose parents had died on the trail. So she decided to open an orphanage in Oregon. After a few years, it evolved into Pacific University, one of the first liberal arts colleges in the region. Today, the school boasts a student body of 1,800 and a national reputation for programs in psychology and optometry.

Tabitha would have been proud of the university's success, but she probably would have dismissed any praise for her accomplishments. She tended to pass the credit to a higher power.

"God had a work for me to do," she once wrote, "and had seen fit to use me to accomplish His own purposes."

Faith was a driving force throughout Tabitha's life, which began May 1, 1780, in Brimfield, Massachusetts. At the age of nineteen, she married an Episcopal clergyman, Clark Brown. He died eighteen years later, leaving her to raise their three children alone. To support her family, she taught school in Maryland, Virginia, and Missouri.

Tabitha's oldest son, Orus, was among the adventurous Americans who made the original "Great Migration" to Oregon in 1843. After spending a year on the Tualatin Plains about twenty-five miles west of present-day Portland, he hustled back to Missouri to extol the "paradise" he'd found. He persuaded Tabitha, his sister and her family, and his uncle, Captain Brown, to join him in the West.

The families embarked by wagon train from St. Charles, Missouri, on April 15, 1846. The expedition went smoothly until the group passed Fort Hall, in what is now southeastern Idaho. There, Tabitha later said, a "rascally fellow" persuaded them to take a newly discovered shortcut, a route that would lead them across the southern Cascades and avoid the difficult trip through the Blue Mountains and the Columbia River valley. But the emigrants soon realized they had taken a shortcut to trouble. As Tabitha recalled:

> Our sufferings from that time no tongue can tell. We had sixty miles of desert without grass or water, mountains to climb, cattle giving out, wagons breaking, emigrants sick and dying, hostile Indians to guard against by night and by day. We were carried south of Oregon hundreds of miles into Utah Territory and California; fell in with the Clamotte (Klamath) and Rogue River Indians; lost nearly all of our cattle.

Tabitha and her brother-in-law reached Salem on Christmas Day 1846. A Methodist missionary invited them to stay with his family until they could get established. It was the first time they had been inside a house in more than eight months. Tabitha did domestic chores to earn room and board for herself and Captain Brown. The plucky grandmother had little choice; she had lost almost everything she owned on the trip, including her bed and rocking chair. All she had were a few clothes and a small coin called a picayune, which she discovered in the finger of a glove. It was worth only a fraction more than six cents.

Tabitha used the money to buy three sewing needles and traded some of her clothes to Indian women for buckskin. She began to make rugged leather gloves, which she sold to loggers and other pioneers who worked hard with their hands. Before long, she had managed to saved thirty dollars.

Although she was rallying financially, Tabitha never really wanted the money for herself. She dreamed of founding an orphanage, a refuge for homeless children.

In the fall of 1847, she was visiting her son Orus in Forest Grove when she was invited to a Presbyterian church meeting. There, she met the Reverend and Mrs. Harvey Clark, missionaries from New York who had come to Oregon in 1840. The Clarks asked Tabitha to spend the winter with them, an invitation she gratefully accepted.

"Our intimacy ever since has been more like that of mother and children than strangers," Tabitha wrote later. "They are about the same age as my own children, and look to me for advice."

Tabitha also wanted advice. She told the Reverend Clark about her desire to start an orphanage. In her memoirs, she recalled the following conversation:

> I said to Mr. Clark: "Why has Providence frowned on me and left me poor in this world? Had He blessed me with riches as he has many others, I know right well what I would do."
>
> "What would you do?" was his question.
>
> "I would establish myself in a comfortable house and receive all poor children and be a mother to them."
>
> He fixed his keen eyes upon me to see if I was candid in what I said.
>
> "Yes I am."
>
> "If so," he replied, "I will try and see what efforts we can make."

Clark was able to sell other church members on the idea. They agreed to build a log boarding house at Forest Grove and provide food and other supplies. Tabitha opened the doors of the orphanage in 1848. For the first year, she worked for free. She also worked hard; housekeeping, sewing, gardening, and cooking were but a few of the tasks that needed her attention.

"I managed (the children), did almost all my own work but the washing, which was always done by the scholars," she recalled in her memoirs. In one five-month period, she mixed 3,425 pounds of flour into bread.

Initially, Tabitha supervised thirty boarders ranging in age from four to twenty-one. Not all of them were orphans. Some had been left behind by parents who had rushed to the California gold fields in hopes of finding a fortune. Those parents who could afford it paid a dollar a week per child for board and tuition.

Tabitha was popular with her charges, and they called her "Grandma." She wore white caps trimmed with pillow lace and was "exceedingly quiet and cheerful in her ways," according to Jane Kinney Smith, who lived as a child at the bustling orphanage. So "orderly and intelligent" was Grandma's management that Smith couldn't remember a single discipline problem. She later recalled the experience:

> In the mornings, especially Sundays, [Tabitha] would waken her household by singing, and as her voice was still sweet and strong, and her singing good, this made the children feel cheerful all the week. This lady also was something of a mechanic, and contrived many conveniences, one being a clay-made oven, which was the admiration of the neighborhood; having been constructed by simply a wooden framework, of proper size, over which was placed a sufficiency of well-mixed clay, after which the woodwork was burned out, and other fuel added until the clay was hardened into something like brick.

Another student, Marcus Walker, remembered that Tabitha had a "stern face and dignified bearing, but we knew that behind them lay the kindest heart that ever befriended a homeless orphan."

By 1851, forty children were enrolled at Tualatin Academy, as the school was called. Three years later, the territorial legislature decreed that it could become Pacific University, but it continued to serve children until 1914.

Despite her key role in founding the university, Tabitha was not among its ten original trustees. They were all men, which was not uncommon in those days, when women did not even have the right to vote. But strong-willed Tabitha would not be deterred from playing an active role on campus.

The university's first president, Sidney Harper Marsh, was an Eastern transplant who had to teach classes as well as run the school. He had no house or office, so he fashioned a makeshift home in the unfinished upper story of the science hall. He balanced his bed on trestles that he laid across the floor joists. To reach it each evening, he climbed a ladder. Marsh was discouraged at times by these primitive conditions, and he sought Tabitha when he needed a pep talk. "The good soul would cheer him up and bid him take heart," the *Oregon Sunday Journal* of Portland reported in 1909.

An oak tree graced the middle of the campus in those days. When it was hot, Tabitha, a familiar sight in her white cap and calico dress, would often take refuge in the shade beneath its branches, a book propped open in her lap, her cane lying beside her. She identified with the gnarled old tree because it was aged and crippled, just as she was. The hollow trunk also once sheltered a swarm of bees. When Tabitha died, a plaque was nailed to the oak proclaiming it "Grandma Tabitha's Bee Tree."

The oak has long since toppled, but a petrified stump marks the site of the academy's original log cabin. A plaque memorializes the building and Tabitha's contributions.

Old College Hall, built in 1850, still stands on campus. Tabitha raised money to buy the building materials and supervised meals for

PACIFIC UNIVERSITY ARCHIVES

Old College Hall

the settlers who erected it in only two days. A few years later, the
Union Army recruited soldiers for the Civil War on the steps of the
building. Now listed on the National Register of Historic Places,
Old College Hall is the oldest building west of the Rocky Mountains that has been used continuously for educational purposes. The
wooden structure has been renovated so that it looks as it did in the
mid-nineteenth century. It is still used for classes, and the second
floor houses a museum that celebrates the history of the university
and Tabitha's life.

Tabitha helped the university and the community in other ways,
both large and small. In the fall of 1855, several Indian tribes in the
region were fuming over the encroachment of settlers and miners on
their homelands. The people of Forest Grove feared an attack. Tabitha
slogged up and down the muddy paths of town, recruiting men and
boys to dig a trench around Old College Hall as a defense. A sentry
also was dispatched to the hall's cupola, from which he could see

three miles in every direction.

Meanwhile, Tabitha and some of her students set to work sewing an American flag. On it, they arranged twenty stars in the shape of one large five-pointed star. Around the edges, they stitched in narrow letters the words: "Co. 'D' FIRST OREGON VOLUNTEERS 1855–56." According to family lore, Tabitha tore up one of her own petticoats to make the flag because fabric was scarce.

Forest Grove never was attacked by Indians, but the company carried the flag when it took part in the Yakima Indian War of 1855 and the Bannock Indian campaign of 1878. Today, the flag is kept at the university museum.

In 1854, when Tabitha was seventy-four years old, university officials asked her to help the financially strapped school by traveling to the East Coast to solicit donations from Christian groups. She turned them down, pointing out that she was simply too old and frail to make the trip cross-country. But because she was thrifty, she had saved money to buy cattle and property. She donated some of this to the university for an endowment just before she died on May 4, 1858, three days after her seventy-eighth birthday. She was buried in Pioneer Cemetery in Salem.

Ella Brown Spooner, who wrote two short books on Tabitha's exploits, described her feisty grandmother as selfless and dedicated. "Instead of pursuing happiness, she allowed it to come to her when she was busy lending a hand. Wherever she went she was held in high esteem."

Almost a century and a half after Tabitha's death, Oregonians still appreciate her indomitable spirit. In 1987, the state legislature proclaimed her the "Mother Symbol of Oregon," saying that she "represents the distinctive pioneer heritage and the charitable and compassionate nature of Oregon's people."

Tabitha herself said she would leave it to others to appraise her life and legacy. Three years before she died, she wrote to relatives:

You must be judges whether I have been doing good or evil. I have labored for myself and the rising generation, but I have now quit hard work, and live at my ease, independent as to worldly concerns. I have a nicely furnished white frame house on a lot in town, within a short distance of the public buildings.... I have eight other lots, without buildings, worth $150 each. I have eight cows and a number of young cattle. The cows I rent out for their milk.... I have rising $1,100 cash due me; $400 of it I have donated to the university, besides $100 I gave the academy three years ago. This much I have been able to accumulate by my own industry, independent of my children, since I drew $6\frac{1}{4}$ cents from the finger of my glove. ⚜

Abigail Scott Duniway

1834-1915

Path Breaker

Twelve-year-old Jenny Scott's heart ached as she stood at her mother's bedside. She had just watched the weary woman give birth for the tenth time in sixteen years. Now Mrs. Scott cradled her newborn daughter in her arms and wept tears not of joy but of anguish. "Poor baby!" she moaned. "She'll be a woman someday. Poor baby! A woman's lot is so hard!"

The scene reminded Jenny of her tenth birthday, when her mother had confided that Jenny's own birth in 1834 had been a sorrow "almost too grievous to be borne." Anne Roelofson Scott had wept then, too. The birth of a girl, in her mind, was no cause for celebration. She had lost her own vitality to the endless toil of frontier life and the strain of frequent pregnancies. She assumed her daughters were destined to suffer similar fates.

Jenny never forgot her mother's hopeless words, nor her mother's helplessness to improve her lot in life. Haunted by these memories, she committed herself to the fight for women's rights—and in doing so became one of the most important women in the history of Oregon.

Abigail Jane Scott—friends and relatives called her Jenny—was born on October 22, 1834, in a humble farmhouse on the

Abigail Scott Duniway

Illinois frontier. She was the third of a dozen children born to Anne and John Tucker Scott. Her father was a strong, generous, and adventurous man who believed wholeheartedly in the motto "Hard work never hurt anybody." Her mother was a self-sacrificing, sweet-tempered woman whose early death disproved his belief.

Abigail's first year of life was especially difficult for the Scotts. Torrential rains and flooding followed by severe drought destroyed their crops. So the family had to rely more than usual on the money Anne Scott earned selling eggs, butter, and needlework. With her mother "worn ...to a frazzle with such drudgery," baby Jenny got little attention. She spent her first summer, she later wrote, sitting on the floor "complaining and neglected, soothed only by a piece of bacon, attached by a string to a bed-post."

Abigail had to assume some of the burden of frontier farming when she was still very young. One of her earliest memories was of standing on a chair to wash dirty dishes with harsh, handmade soap. She picked and spun wool and peeled and quartered apples for drying. As she grew older, she churned butter, chopped wood, milked cows, hoed fields, and scrubbed clothes on a washboard. At the age of nine, while resodding a lawn that had been damaged by drought, she suffered a back injury that would plague her for the rest of her life.

Abigail grew quickly into a tall, spindly, awkward child with a strong will but a fragile constitution. She was often ill and, as a result, managed to attend school only for a few scattered months. Her busy mother somehow found time to teach her to read, spell, and recite rhymes. Abigail began to write "poesy," some of which was published in the local newspaper.

In 1852, when Abigail was seventeen, John Scott succumbed to "Oregon fever." The bug had bitten him more than a decade earlier, when he had attended a speech by Jason Lee, the enthusiastic Methodist missionary to the Pacific Northwest. Lee had extolled the beauty of the Oregon Territory and stressed the importance of American settlers laying claim to it before the British. Although Anne Scott was weak from caring for her nine surviving children and slaving dawn to dusk at her countless household tasks, her husband decreed that the family would make the long and dangerous journey west over the Oregon Trail. Amid tears and protests, the family set out on April 2 in five covered wagons packed with only their most essential belongings. Abigail smuggled a treasured spelling book in the bottom of her sewing bag.

For six months, the family crawled 2,400 miles across the plains and mountains with a train of other emigrants. At first, Abigail thought the trip was fun. After all, it offered a release from the drudgery of farm life. Her father had assigned her the job of keeping a travel diary. So while her mother and sisters cooked the evening meal, she sat with pen and paper, recording the day's events. She dutifully noted the forts they passed, the rivers they forded, and the condition of the grass for the cattle and horses, but she was especially impressed by the scenery, which she found "grand," "romantic," "picturesque and sublime."

It wasn't long before tears stained the pages of Abigail's journal. On June 20, as the caravan neared Fort Laramie, Wyoming, she wrote, "How mysterious are the works of an all-wise and overruling Providence! We little thought when last Sabbath's pleasant sun shed upon us his congenial rays that when the next should come it would find us mourning over the sickness and death of our beloved Mother!"

Poor, work-worn Anne Scott had been too frail to resist an outbreak of cholera among the emigrants. One day she was well; the next she was gone. The family scratched a shallow grave in a hillside ablaze with wildflowers, then covered it with stones to protect the body from hungry wolves. Abigail's younger sister Harriet later recalled that they "heaped and covered mother's grave with beautiful wild roses, so the cruel stones were hid from view."

On August 28, near what is now Durkee, Oregon, tragedy struck yet again. This time its victim was Abigail's three-year-old brother, Willie. "The ruthless monster death not yet content, has once more entered our fold & taken in his icy grasp the treasure of our hearts!" Abigail wrote. "Last night our darling Willie was called from earth, to vie with angels around the throne of God." He had died, she said, of "cholera infantum, or dropsy of the brain."

During the final month of the journey, as the family crossed the Cascades, Abigail's diary was tinged with disenchantment. She wrote of hunger, lost cattle, worn-out shoes, and crippled wagons. Finally, on September 28—penniless, exhausted, and grieving—the Scotts reached the Willamette Valley and the home of maternal relatives. "We found them all in good health and well satisfied," she noted in her last journal entry. "They were of course glad to see us."

Despite her lack of formal education, Abigail soon managed to get a job as a teacher in what is now Eola, a tiny community six miles west of Salem. The spelling book she'd smuggled across two-thirds of the continent came in handy as she crammed to learn what she would teach her students the next day.

As Abigail's career blossomed, so too did her social life. One of the main attractions of the Oregon Territory was the Donation Land Act of 1850, which entitled every married man to a sizable tract of free land. He could claim an equal amount in his wife's name, so unattached women—what few there were in the region—were coveted prizes. Ranchers, lumberjacks, and teamsters scoured the countryside for brides in what one historian referred to as "the most serious epidemic of marriage fever in American history."

Suddenly besieged by suitors, Abigail had no intention of becoming a "land bride," wooed only for the acreage she could bring to a union. She had nothing but scorn for those shameless men who proposed indiscriminately "to tearful widows of a fortnight and little girls dirty with mud pies." Cautiously, she favored Benjamin Duniway, a tall, good-natured rancher four years her senior. When they married in August 1853, she recalled so vividly her mother's servile existence that she purged the wedding ceremony of the word "obey."

Since Ben had not married within a year of reaching Oregon, he wasn't eligible for a land claim in his wife's name, but he did own 320 acres in untamed Clackamas County. So now, little more than a year after leaving the grind of the Scott farm, Abigail found herself stuck on her husband's meager homestead. For the next four years, she washed, scrubbed, churned, cooked, and nursed her first two babies, Clara and Willis. Bachelors in the neighborhood—and there were many—got in the habit of flocking to her home at mealtime, hoping for a good home-cooked stew or a slice of fresh-baked pie. Hospitable Ben always invited them to pull up an extra chair and stay awhile.

Abigail resented the extra work these freeloaders created and derisively dubbed her cabin "Free Hotel." Decades later, in her autobiography *Path Breaking*, she wrote bitterly of those "monotonous years":

> To bear two children in two and a half years from my marriage day, to make thousands of pounds of butter every year for market; . . . to sew and cook and wash and iron; to bake and clean and stew and fry; to be, in short, a general pioneer drudge, with never a penny of my own, was not pleasant business for an erstwhile school teacher, who had earned a salary that had not gone before marriage, as did her butter and eggs and chickens afterwards, for groceries, and to pay taxes or keep up the wear and tear of horseshoeing, plow-sharpening and harness-mending. My recreation during those monotonous years was wearing out my wedding clothes, or making over for my cherished babies the bridal outfit I had earned as a school teacher.

Eventually, Ben abandoned his barren acreage on the fringe of the wilderness. In 1857, he acquired a more fertile tract in Yamhill County, where he hoped to establish a fruit orchard. Abigail found herself cooking and cleaning for a batch of hired hands. She could barely afford to take time out to give birth to two more sons, Hubert and Wilkie. To her dismay, she was following in her mother's weary footsteps, but she took some comfort from the fact that her husband was "sober, industrious, and kind" and her marriage "more than usually harmonious."

Besides, Abigail had grown up with the idea that a woman's lot was, in her words, to "engage in a lifetime of unpaid servitude and personal sacrifice."

"I was filling my Heaven-appointed sphere," she later wrote, "for which final recompense awaited me in the land of souls."

Desperate for intellectual stimulation, Abigail again turned to writing. She began with lively letters and articles for the weekly *Oregon Argus*. In 1859, when she was twenty-five, she had a book published. Entitled *Captain Gray's Company, or Crossing the Plains and Living in Oregon*, it was a novel based on her own experiences on the Oregon Trail. Reviewers called it "silly" and scoffed at its bad grammar. One critic was "hugely disgusted with its general lack of good taste." But for all its faults, it gave Abigail her first claim to fame: It was the first novel ever printed commercially in Oregon.

Two years after Abigail's plunge into the literary world, Ben made a decision that pitched his family into crisis. Abigail was busy plucking ducks one day with the intention of making feather pillows when she saw an acquaintance approach Ben as he was working at the woodpile. She overheard the man ask Ben to co-sign a business loan. The arrangement would make Ben responsible for repaying the loan if the man could not.

Abigail cringed. A transaction like that could spell financial ruin for the Duniways! Shouldn't she have a say in something that could affect her family so adversely? But this was business, and business was the domain of men. She bit her lip and hoped for the best.

This time the best was not to be. The fledgling business was destroyed in a flood, and the sheriff soon came knocking at the Duniways' door, demanding repayment of the loan. There was nothing they could do but sell the farm and use the proceeds to pay off the debt. In 1863, devastated by their bad luck, they moved to a small house they owned in the nearby town of Lafayette.

With four children now to provide for, Ben went to work hauling freight with his team and wagon. Abigail tried to do her part by operating a small school, but fate had not yet finished with the Duniways. Soon after their move, Ben's team of horses bolted, knocked him to the ground, and dragged a heavy wagon over him. He spent the rest of his life as an invalid, incapable of supporting his family.

Suddenly, Abigail was forced to be the family breadwinner as well as homemaker. She enlarged her school and converted the loft of their home into a dormitory for female boarders. The workload was overwhelming, as she later recalled:

I would rise from my bed at 3 o'clock in Summer and 4 o'clock in Winter, to do a day's work before school time. Then, repairing to my school room I would teach the primer classes while resting at my desk. For two hours afterwards I would occupy the time with the older students....

I would prepare the table for luncheon in the dining room before repairing to the school room; and, returning to lessons at 1 o'clock P.M., would resume school work until 4 o'clock, before taking up my household duties again in the home. And yet, notwithstanding all this effort, I led an easier life than I had known on a pioneer farm....

After about a year, Abigail had saved enough money to move her family to Albany, a larger and livelier town on the Willamette River. She sold her school at a profit and opened a millinery shop. It was the only profession other than teaching that was considered "respectable" for a woman.

It was as a storekeeper that Abigail learned how unjustly the law treated women. As she fitted hats, she offered a sympathetic ear to customers down on their luck. On one occasion, the wife of a well-to-do farmer begged her for sewing work because her husband had bought a racehorse with the money she'd saved selling butter. Now she couldn't afford coats for her daughters to wear to Sunday school.

On another occasion, a "faded little over-worked mother of half a dozen children" came to Abigail in distress. Her husband had just sold their household belongings and vanished with the money. The desperate woman knew of a family about to leave town who would rent her their house and sell her their furniture for a reasonable price.

"If I could borrow the money in a lump sum," she pleaded, "I could repay it in installments. Then I could keep my children together, with the aid of a few boarders."

Abigail arranged for a charitable friend to loan the woman the money. All was well until, one day, the derelict husband returned. He refused to acknowledge his wife's debt and sold all the new furniture. In the eyes of the law, he had every right. His wife couldn't borrow money legally without his consent, and any property she owned was his to do with as he pleased. The couple eventually divorced, and the woman lost custody of her children.

On yet another occasion, Abigail loaned a woman the supplies she needed to open a millinery shop in another town. The woman's husband, Abigail explained, was a "well-meaning but irresponsible fellow, noted chiefly for poverty."

One day a stranger came to collect on a debt the woman's husband had incurred before their marriage. Since her husband was unable to pay, the creditor seized all the woman's merchandise, forcing her to close her business.

Abigail brooded over these injustices. With laws as they were, women were at the mercy of their husbands. One evening, after dinner, she poured out her frustration.

"Ben," she complained, "one-half of the women are dolls, the rest of them are drudges, and we're all fools!"

Idly stroking her hair, he replied, "Don't you know it will never be any better for women until they vote?"

Abigail felt as if someone had lit a fire inside her."The light permeated the very marrow of my bones," she later recalled, "filling me with such hope, courage, and determination as no obstacle could conquer and nothing but death could overcome."

Abigail was ready to take on the world as a crusader for women's suffrage. She began in November 1870 by joining with two friends to form the Oregon State Equal Suffrage Association. Next, she moved her family to Portland and founded *The New Northwest*, a weekly newspaper that, for the next sixteen years, would serve as a forum for her feminist views.

She was able to get some journalistic guidance from her younger brother, Harvey, who was editor of the Portland-based newspaper, the *Oregonian*. She also had the blessing of her husband and the support of her children, whom she one day would describe as her "highest achievement and principal asset." While her older sons helped set type and print the newspaper, daughter Clara kept house and managed the millinery shop. Ben returned to work as a part-time clerk with the Portland customs house, a humble and unde-manding job he got with the help of his brother-in-law. He also tended the youngest boys, Clyde and Ralph, who had been born in Albany during the late 1860s. It was he who nursed them when they were ill, gave them their baths, and entertained them at bedtime with stories and songs. His children adored him for his tenderness. Their feelings for their mother were more ambivalent. Certainly they respected her for her ambition and accomplishments, but they re-sented the lack of maternal attention. One of her sons, when he was grown, complained that Abigail "lacked the calmness and patience to deal with the personal needs of ailing children."

Abigail was careful not to use *The New Northwest* as a grindstone for too many axes. To attract readers throughout Oregon, Washington, and Idaho, she served up a lively mix of crime reports, political exposés, advice columns, fashion hints, and serial fiction. Still, from the outset she let her readers know exactly where she stood. In her debut issue of May 5, 1871, she wrote:

We started out in business with strong prejudices against "strong-minded women." Experience and common sense have conquered those prejudices. We see, under the existing customs of society, one half of the women over-taxed and underpaid; hopeless yet struggling toilers in the world's drudgery; while the other half are frivolous, idle and expensive. Both of these conditions of society are wrong. Both have resulted from women's lack of political and consequent pecuniary and moral responsibility. To prove this, and to elevate women, that thereby herself and son and brother man may be benefitted and the world made better, purer, and happier, is the aim of this publication.

A few months after founding her newspaper, Abigail launched in earnest her campaign for suffrage. She invited Susan B. Anthony to travel to Portland from San Francisco, where the nation's foremost feminist had lately been stumping for women's rights. Anthony agreed to a two-month lecture tour of Oregon and Washington, with Abigail as her manager and publicist. The pair crisscrossed the region by stagecoach and steamer, stopping to speak in churches, schools, saloons, barns, private homes—anywhere they could gather an audience for their message. When Anthony finished the tour and returned to the East Coast, Abigail continued on her own to carry "the gospel of equal rights" throughout the Pacific Northwest.

For the next several years, Abigail traveled three to five days a week, penning articles and editorials while on the move and mailing them back to *The New Northwest*. She was a persistent crusader. In 1886 alone, she gave 181 lectures; traveled 3,000 miles by stage, rail, steamer, buggy, buckboard, and on foot; and wrote 400 columns for her paper—all the while soliciting new subscriptions in every town she visited. In her spare time, she scribbled novels, at least one of which was published, featuring downtrodden women who either succumbed to overbearing men or asserted their independence.

Often Abigail's equal-rights message was not well-received. Many men were threatened by the idea of sharing political power with women, while some society dames, content upon their pedestals, were reluctant to tinker with the status quo. But Abigail believed that equality for women was important to the welfare of both sexes.

"Women who seek the ballot for liberty's sake are not proposing to govern men," she explained. "We are seeking for an opportunity to govern ourselves. We ask nothing but our right to use our voices, as [men's] companions and co-workers, in making the laws which we are taxed to maintain, to which we, equally with [men], are held amenable."

Abigail counted on logic, passion, and wit to convert people to her cause. Once, when she was traveling by stage to Yakima, Washington, a fellow passenger taunted her about suffrage to the amusement of his traveling companions.

"Madam," he said, "you ought to be at home enjoying yourself, like my wife's doing. I want to bear all the hardships of life myself and let her sit by the fire toasting her footsies."

When the stage reached Yakima, the driver stopped to let the man off at his own front gate. There, in his snow-covered yard, stood his wife, busily chopping firewood. As the man climbed from the coach, Abigail called after him, "I see your wife is toasting her footsies!" From then on, the man was known to his chums as "Old Footsie Toaster."

Sometimes Abigail allowed her quick temper to get the best of her. She could be tactless and combative when responding to opponents. Once, she described a California man who had voted against women's suffrage as "California's greatest curse and deepest shame," a "blatant blatherskite," a "worthless alien cur," a "truckling coward," and a "brazen braggart" with a "following of corner loafers, midnight ruffians, sand-bag garroters, flannel-mouthed bog-trotters and adulterous political preachers."

When the editor of a Pacific Northwest newspaper claimed that his "estimate of womanhood [was] too high to ... aid in an effort to drag her down to the filthy pool of party politics," Abigail shot back with a militant response:

We have waited long for our brothers, who have made the filth, to arise in their boasted might and cleanse and purify their politics.... The reeking political slime in which they daily writhe calls aloud to us for purification. Women have harkened to the call, and ... woman, with her scrubbing brushes, her dustpan, her soap suds and her ready-waiting raiment of cleanliness, is baring her arms and fortifying her "constitution" to come to the rescue.

In 1872, Abigail persuaded the Oregon legislature to consider suffrage legislation for the first time. The bill was defeated by a narrow margin, but as a consolation prize lawmakers passed the Sole Trader Bill. It protected the holdings of businesswomen from seizure by their husbands' creditors. In 1878—with the grand prize of suffrage still eluding her—Abigail helped secure passage of the Married Woman's Property Act, which permitted wives to hold property and earn wages of their own.

As the suffrage movement continued to sweep the Pacific Northwest, another movement spearheaded by women was also gaining a foothold. In 1874, a group of angry Midwestern wives and mothers had formed the Women's Christian Temperance Union (WCTU). Their goal originally was to encourage self-control and the moderate use of liquor, but some were beginning to call for its prohibition.

A teetotaler herself, Abigail at first welcomed an alliance with the WCTU. But she soon became alarmed by talk of prohibition, which represented a loss of individual rights—the very antithesis of what the suffrage movement was all about. In her opinion, prohibition was "intolerance and quackery." She believed in discouraging the use of liquor through taxation, education, regulation, and ridicule—not by banning the sale of liquor altogether.

Women's suffrage, she said, "will prove in time the magic key to … enable women to rear a race of men who will be voluntarily free from drunkenness, because a race of free, enlightened mothers will naturally produce a race of free, enlightened sons."

Meanwhile, she argued, let's not alienate men—who, after all, hold the power to grant women the right to vote—by threatening to use that vote to deprive them of their whiskey. To do so, she said, would be like "driving nails into the closed coffin lid of … women's liberties."

Abigail withdrew her support from the temperance movement, infuriating her former allies in the WCTU. They accused her of selling out to liquor, of being a closet drinker, and of disgracing the cause of women's suffrage. When she tried to speak against prohibition at a national convention, she was rebuked even by her colleague

Susan B. Anthony. Oregon suffragists urged her to withdraw from the campaign because she had become too controversial.

Life on the home front had become equally distressing. In January 1886, Abigail's beloved daughter Clara died of tuberculosis at the age of thirty-one. Ben's health, too, had taken a turn for the worse. He decided, along with several of their sons, to buy a cattle ranch in Idaho, in the hope that outdoor living and country air would be more invigorating.

Grief-stricken and discouraged, Abigail sold *The New Northwest* and followed her family to Idaho. It was "like parting with a loved and trusted child," she later said. She helped cope with her sorrow by immersing herself for the next seven years in the battle for suffrage in Idaho. Her impassioned speeches helped to make it, in 1896, the first of the three Pacific Northwest states to enfranchise women.

Abigail's first big victory was tarnished by the death that same year of her husband Ben. Ailing and alone, but inspired by her experience in Idaho, she threw herself back into the fight for suffrage in Oregon, having returned with Ben to Portland in 1894. The state legislature had defeated suffrage bills in every session since 1872, and Abigail watched in frustration as they continued to do the same in the first decade of the new century. Some blamed the record number of defeats on Abigail's antagonistic ways and "errors in judgment." Abigail blamed them, at least in part, on her brother Harvey and his powerful newspaper, the *Oregonian*, which had been the only major paper in the state to oppose women's suffrage, on the grounds that ignorant voters were dangerous and most women were uneducated. When Harvey died in 1910, the *Oregonian* withdrew its opposition, and the path to victory lay clear at last.

In November 1912, a few days after Abigail's seventy-eighth birthday, Oregon by a narrow margin became the ninth state to recognize the right of women to vote. Governor Oswald West invited Abigail, as the "architect of woman's suffrage in Oregon," to sign the official proclamation. Deaf, overweight, crippled with arthritis, and confined to a wheelchair, the fiery crusader, once hated and feared, had become "the Grand Old Woman of Oregon."

Abigail died at the age of eighty on October 11, 1915—five years before ratification of a national suffrage amendment. After a lifetime of "toil, hardship, privation, ridicule, sneers, and vituperation," she was able, as she had always wished, to "enter heaven a free angel." ❧

Abigail Scott Duniway voting

BETHENIA OWENS-ADAIR

1840–1926

Doctor in Petticoats

Bethenia Owens winced as she watched the bumbling doctor try repeatedly and unsuccessfully to insert a catheter into his young patient. The ailing child's mother had summoned her that evening in 1870 because of her reputation as a capable—if untrained—nurse. Now, Bethenia could no longer tolerate the little girl's cries of pain. When the doctor put down the catheter to wipe a smudge from his glasses, Bethenia didn't hesitate to grab her opportunity.

"Let me try, Doctor," she later recalled saying as she snatched the instrument. Before he could object, she inserted it "with perfect ease."

The "tortured child," she noted, felt "immediate relief," while the sobbing mother embraced her gratefully. The humiliated doctor was not impressed. He upbraided her "most emphatically" for interfering with his treatment.

Decades later, when Bethenia could look back smugly at such disapproval, she would attribute this "apparently unimportant incident" with igniting a new ambition: She wanted to become a physician. But first she would have to overcome society's long-standing

Bethenia Owens-Adair

revulsion toward the idea of female doctors.

A medical journal published in 1867 voiced the prevailing attitude of the time when it declared, "We hope never to see the day when female character shall be so completely unsexed, as to fit it for the disgusting duties which imperatively devolve upon one who would attain proficiency, or even respectability, in the healing art." The author of a nineteenth-century medical textbook offered the patronizing opinion that women have "a head almost too small for intellect but just big enough for love."

In other words, medicine was man's work, too nasty, intimate, and taxing for the delicate sensibilities of a woman. Little wonder that in 1870 fewer than one percent of the nation's physicians were female.

Bethenia had spent her lifetime overcoming such prejudices. Already, she had proved stubborn, persistent, and resourceful enough to leave an abusive marriage, build her own business, and support herself and her son. True to her ambition, she would eventually earn two medical degrees and become one of the first women to practice medicine in Oregon. She would also be an advocate of temperance and women's suffrage.

Bethenia Owens—who hyphenated her name to Owens-Adair after marrying her second husband—was born February 7, 1840, in Van Buren County, Missouri. She was the second of nine children of Thomas and Sarah Owens. At the age of three, she traveled west with her family in one of the first emigrant wagon trains to blaze the Oregon Trail. They settled on the Clatsop plain at the mouth of the Columbia River.

Bethenia later remembered her childhood self as "very small and delicate in stature, and of a highly nervous and sensitive nature." At the same time, she said, she "possessed a strong and vigorous constitution, and a most wonderful endurance."

Her favorite playmate was her younger but bigger brother Flem, with whom she competed shamelessly at wrestling and other feats of strength. Looking back on those years, she confessed, "I was a veritable 'tom-boy' and gloried in the fact. It was the regret of my life up to the age of thirty-five years that I was not born a boy, for I realized early in life that a girl was hampered and hemmed in on all sides, simply by the accident of sex."

Although Bethenia relished her reputation for toughness, she also had a tender side. That and her status as one of the oldest Owens girls helped to propel her into the position of "family nurse." She later described the role in her memoir *Dr. Owens-Adair: Some of Her Life Experiences*:

> [I]t was seldom that I had not a child in my arms, and more clinging to me. Where there is a baby every two years, there is always no end of nursing to be done; especially when the mother's time is occupied, as it was then, every moment, from early morning till late at night, with much outdoor as well as indoor work. [Mother] seldom found time to devote to the baby.

In May 1854, Bethenia started her own family by marrying Legrand Hill, a tall, handsome man who had worked as a farmhand for her father. She was fourteen at the time—not an uncommon age for marriage on the frontier—and she was so petite she could stand upright under her husband's outstretched arm. She bore a son, George, two years later.

It wasn't long after the wedding that Bethenia realized she had made a horrible mistake. Her husband was not a good provider. He preferred reading novels and hunting to working on the 320-acre farm that he had bought for them on credit. Bethenia had to keep house in a crude log cabin with no floor or chimney—because Hill never got around to building them.

"He simply idled away his time," she later said, "doing a day's work now and then, spending more than he made." Worse yet, Hill proved to be quick-tempered and even brutal, especially after the birth of their son.

"Our trouble usually started over the baby," Bethenia lamented. "He was such a sickly, tiny mite, with an abnormal, voracious appetite, but his father thought him old enough to be trained and disciplined, and would spank him unmercifully because he cried." When she tried to intervene, she said, Hill would strike and choke her.

By 1859, Bethenia could endure no more. "Broken in spirit and health," she filed for a divorce—a disgraceful solution in those days. She reclaimed her maiden name but refused to accept the charity of relatives. Deep within her, a fiercely independent spirit was stirring. She would earn a living for herself and her son by picking berries, cleaning, nursing, and taking in washing, ironing, and sewing. She even briefly taught school, despite having completed only three months of formal education herself.

"Of my sixteen scholars there were three further advanced than myself," she later confessed, "but I took their books home with me nights, and with the help of my brother-in-law, I managed to prepare the lessons beforehand, and they never suspected my incompetency."

By now, Bethenia was convinced that the only way to ensure a brighter future for herself and her son was to improve her own education. She moved to Astoria, enrolled in school, and, to her horror, was "placed in the primary class!"

"Words cannot express my humiliation," she said, "at having to recite with children eight and ten years old!" To her relief, she made swift progress.

By studying as she worked—often propping an open textbook beside her ironing board or washtub—Bethenia succeeded in qualifying for a teaching certificate. Once again, she worked as a country schoolmarm. When she managed to save $400 in wages, she bought a lot in Astoria and contracted with a carpenter to build her a home of her own. She was proud to have vanquished the "young, ignorant, inexperienced child-mother" who had been neglected and misused by her husband. She judged herself now to be a "full-grown, self-reliant woman," ready to take on the world.

Partly at the urging of family members, Bethenia returned to Roseburg in 1867 and opened a millinery and dressmaking shop. For two years, she prospered at this new endeavor. Then a more experienced milliner moved to town and opened a shop next door. Bethenia's business suffered from the competition, but she was not about to accept defeat. In an autobiographical sketch she wrote for *The Centennial History of Oregon*, she recalled the turning point in her millinery career:

> One beautiful day I was thinking the matter over while eating my dinner in front of a window which overlooked my neighbor's kitchen. I had seen her husband unload several boxes of old hats the evening before, and now they were getting ready for bleaching and pressing. They sat at a table out in the sun on which they placed two new plaster of paris hat blocks, and now the work began not twenty feet from me. My house was above them and I could see them and hear everything they said; but they could not see me. For an hour I sat there and learned the art of cleaning, stiffening, shaping, pressing and bleaching [hats]. Oh, what a revolution. . . . In less than twenty-four hours I had found and held the key to that mysterious knowledge that had charmed away my customers. I commenced at once to put my acquired knowledge into practice and resolved not to allow a soul to know how I had obtained it.

Business flourished again, and Bethenia's rival left town in disgust, never knowing that she had inadvertently revitalized her competition. Bethenia managed to earn $1,500 in her first year as a milliner—a tidy profit for the place and time—but she didn't allow economic security to lull her into complacency. In 1870, after sending her son off to college in California, she began to harbor dreams of getting a medical education.

"I had always had a fondness for nursing," she later explained, "and had developed such a special capacity in that direction by assisting my neighbors in illness....Mother said I was born a doctor, was always feeding my rag dolls with a spoon."

A few days after her run-in with the catheter-wielding doctor, she borrowed a copy of *Gray's Anatomy* from a sympathetic physician. She planned to spend the next year or so preparing to enroll in a medical school in the East. She arranged for a sister to manage her millinery business.

But her unorthodox decision unleashed a storm of opposition. "My family felt that they were disgraced," Bethenia wrote, "and even my own child was influenced and encouraged to think that I was doing him irreparable injury by my course. People sneered and laughed derisively. Most of my friends seemed to consider it their Christian duty to advise against and prevent me taking this 'fatal' step."

The day of her departure stood out painfully in her memory. She later described it:

> The day I left, two friends came to say good-bye. One said, "Well, this beats all! I always did think you were a smart woman, but you must have gone stark crazy to leave such a business and run off on a wild goose chase." I smiled. "You may change your mind when I come back a

physician and charge you more than I have for hats and bonnets." "Not much. You are a good milliner; but I'll never have a woman doctor about me." Choking back the tears, I replied, "Well, time will tell. . . . " Eleven o'clock P.M. arrived at last, and I found myself seated in the California Overland stage, beginning my long journey across the continent. It was a dark and stormy night, and I was the only inside passenger. There was no one to divert my thoughts from myself, or prevent the full realization of the dreary and desolate sense that I was starting out into an untried world alone, with only my own unaided resources to carry me through.

Bethenia indulged herself in "a flood of tears," but then she recalled the parting advice of her friend and attorney, S. F. Chadwick. His words were "sweet solace" to her wounded spirit: "Go ahead. It is in you. Let it come out. You will win."

Bethenia enrolled in the Eclectic School of Medicine in Philadelphia. It had a questionable reputation—it advocated an unconventional kind of medicine called hydropathy, which involved the use of medicated baths and electricity to treat chronic diseases—but it was one of the few medical schools that would accept women. She graduated a year later in 1874 and was on her way to Portland to set up a private practice when she stopped in Roseburg to visit family. While there, she received a most unusual invitation.

Several local doctors had decided to conduct an autopsy on a derelict old man who had recently died. One of them—the very doctor whose catheter she had commandeered—suggested that they put her in her place by inviting her to attend. Naturally, she would have to decline—the dissection of a man's body was no sight for a proper lady.

To the shock and dismay of the doctors, Bethenia accepted.

Boldly, she shouldered her way through a crowd to reach the shed where the autopsy was to take place. About fifty men and boys had gathered to watch the spectacle. Now they focused their attention on this new novelty: a physician in petticoats.

Bethenia later described in detail the reaction of the doctors to her arrival:

> I opened the door and walked in, went forward and shook hands with Dr. Hoover who advanced to meet me and said, "The operation is to be on the genital organs." I answered, "One part of the body should be as sacred to a physician as another." Dr. Palmer stepped back and said, "I object to a woman being present at a male autopsy. If she is allowed to remain, I will retire." "I came by written invitation" [Bethenia replied] "and I will leave it to a vote whether I go or stay; but first I will ask Dr. Palmer the difference between a woman attending a male autopsy and a man attending a female autopsy?"

When the other doctors said they had no objection to her presence, Dr. Palmer—the catheter bungler—left in a huff. Bethenia had weathered the first crisis of her medical career, but another was close behind. One of the doctors offered her his instruments and suggested that she perform the autopsy herself. Startled, Bethenia complied, and while she worked, the shameful news spread throughout town.

"When I passed out and down to my home, the street was lined with men, women, and children anxious to get a look at the terrible creature," she said. "The women were shocked and scandalized, and the men were disgusted and some amused at the good joke on the doctors." In retrospect, she said, all that saved her from a coat of tar and feathers was the presence in town of her loyal, sharp-shooter brothers.

Bethenia continued to Portland, where she earned enough money from a private practice to send her son to medical school at Willamette University. She also adopted and provided schooling for the daughter of a deceased patient and financed a sister's college education.

Having met her familial obligations, Bethenia decided she could afford to "treat" herself to a bona fide medical education. At the age of thirty-eight, she enrolled at the University of Michigan Medical School, and she received her second medical degree two years later.

After a summer of clinical work in Chicago, six months of postgraduate study in Michigan, and a tour of hospitals in Europe, Bethenia returned to Portland to specialize in diseases of the eye and ear. Although few men were willing to be her patients, her income soon reached a respectable $7,000 a year. She had amply demonstrated that a woman could be a competent and successful physician.

Closely linked with Bethenia's professional career was her commitment to the causes of temperance and women's suffrage. She was active in the Women's Christian Temperance Union and a frequent contributor to the feminist newspaper *The New Northwest*. Its founder, Abigail Scott Duniway, was a friend and ally. By the turn of the century, Bethenia had become a vocal proponent of exercise for women and of sterilizing criminals and the insane.

Although Bethenia had always considered herself "married" to her profession, she decided in 1884 to wed Colonel John Adair, a West Point graduate, farmer, and land developer whom she had known since her youth. The couple adopted two children: her grandson, whose mother had died, and the newborn baby of a patient. They also had a daughter of their own, born in 1887 when Bethenia was forty-seven, but the child lived only a few days. Overcome by grief, the Adairs moved to an isolated farm near Astoria, where for the next eleven years Bethenia divided her time between helping to manage the farm and working as a country doctor. As she later wrote, the latter proved far more demanding than her city practice:

> I carried on my professional work as best I could in that out-of-the-way place; at no time did I ever refuse a call, day or night, rain or shine. I was often compelled to go on foot, through trails so overhung with dense under-growth and obstructed with logs and roots, that a horse and rider could not get past; and through muddy and flooded tide-lands in gum boots.

By 1898, Bethenia suffered from crippling rheumatism. She and her husband moved to North Yakima, Washington, where her son George was practicing medicine, in the hope that the drier climate would help to ease her pain. She lived there until her retirement in 1905, then returned to Oregon to live on the Adair farm near Astoria.

Dr. Bethenia Owens-Adair died of an inflamed heart lining on September 11, 1926. She was eighty-six.

Looking back on her decision to become a doctor, she had once said, "I can assure you it was no laughing matter then to break through the customs, prejudices, and established rules" of the time. But courage, optimism, stamina, and determination had served her well throughout her life. Not only had she ventured where few women had ever dared, but she had blazed a trail that countless others would follow.

"Had I not been inured to hardships and struggles all my life I should have succumbed," she said, "but 'can't' has ever been unknown to me.... I have never flinched from any undertaking and I hope I never shall."

A friend of Bethenia perhaps summed up her nature best when she told her, "If I wished to increase your height by two-and-a-half inches, I would attempt to press you down, and you would grow upward from sheer resentment." ⚜

MARY LEONARD

1845–1912

Lioness of the Law

*T*he "honeymoon" of Daniel and Mary Leonard lasted only about ten days after their marriage on May 19, 1875. It ended, according to Mary, when Daniel refused to give her the large sum of money he had promised her as a wedding gift. She had other complaints about her new husband as well: He expected her to slave in the kitchen of his hotel near The Dalles and cater to his every whim. He abused her mentally and physically and refused to pay her doctor bills when she grew weak from overwork.

Daniel saw the marriage through a different lens. When he filed for divorce in the fall of 1877, he accused Mary of stealing and squandering his money, feigning illness in order to avoid work, denying him his "marital rights," and having an affair with another man.

Mary was not intimidated. When Daniel refused to comply with a judge's order to pay her room and board, she wrote her estranged husband a scathing letter that would later prove incriminating. With characteristically chaotic spelling and punctuation, she wrote:

> [T]o expose what a brute you are I am willing to suffer
> punishment—if you make it necessary.... Do your worse

Mary Leonard

and it will com home to you—I swear it by my life.... I have ever been kind and gentel if treated desent and the most nobel woman might be hardened into a fury when outraged don't fool with a woman like me—beware from ruining me.... beware I say once more and I ask for justice and humanity.

On the morning of January 5, 1878, a few days after Daniel received the letter, his servants were unable to rouse him from his bed. They soon discovered why he was so unresponsive: Someone had shot him in the head with a small-caliber pistol.

Daniel lingered almost two weeks but ultimately died of his wound. The police arrested Mary, and a grand jury indicted her for murder.

Mary had no intention of languishing in a dank cell as she awaited trial. Always persuasive, she cajoled the sheriff into taking her out for walks on bright sunny days. One wide-eyed witness of one of these strolls was a boy named Fred Wilson, who would later become a prominent Oregon judge. He recalled watching Mary sweep by on the arm of the sheriff, a slender woman of average height who was "as good-looking as the majority of women."

Mary went on trial for her life that November. The case against her was flimsy and circumstantial, and her attorney was masterful. The jury quickly ruled that she was not guilty.

Such an ordeal might have prompted most people to avoid further contact with the legal system—but not Mary. Perhaps enamored with the theatrical setting of the courtroom and the dramatic role she had played there, she decided to become an attorney. Seven years after her murder trial, she became the first woman admitted to the Oregon bar. She devoted her legal career to representing the rabble who frequented Portland's municipal courts.

Mary gained quite a reputation among her colleagues, not so

much for her legal skill as for her bombastic style and eccentric behavior. Historian Malcolm Clark Jr. found that her earliest pleadings were:

> … vague and wandering. Her later ones [were] incoherent and even unintelligible. But she had a feminine facility in argument, an inexhaustible fount of words, and boundless enthusiasm. Upon these she relied. She styled herself "Judge" Mary A. Leonard. When the local knights of the green bag gathered of an evening to refresh themselves and replenish their spirits, Mary gathered with them, and, by her own accounting, was as much a man as any.

Mary had come a long way, both literally and figuratively, from her roots. She was born about 1845 in northeastern France to Swiss parents, Johannes and Elisabeth Gysin. Her father worked in a silk mill. She eventually emigrated to the United States and made her way to the Pacific Northwest. Mary apparently was working as a seamstress and domestic servant when she met and married Daniel Leonard.

After Daniel's death, Mary, as his sole heir, collected the money from his estate and left The Dalles. Initially, she used her windfall to open a succession of boarding houses in Portland, but she had higher aspirations. In 1883, she moved to Seattle to study law with a prominent attorney, Colonel J. C. Haines. After eighteen months of his tutelage, she was admitted to the bar in the Washington Territory.

Mary was eager to practice in Oregon, but the men who comprised the state legal profession were not as eager to have her as a colleague. The state supreme court told Mary it could not admit her to the Oregon bar because, as the *Oregonian* reported, "the laws of the state did not confer any authority upon the court to recognize a woman as a duly qualified member of the legal profession."

Mary refused to accept the ruling. She lobbied the state legislature until it amended the law and then returned to the supreme court to get her lawyer's license. This time, the judges told her she had not met a one-year residency requirement. Mary assembled evidence that the one-year rule was not being applied to male applicants, thereby making her the victim of discrimination. She was finally admitted to the Oregon bar in mid-April 1886.

Mary's conflict with the courts was far from over. In fact, as an attorney, temperamental Mary seemed to get into as much legal trouble as did the clients she represented.

One client, a woman named Annie Branson, had sued a fellow named Wickstrom for breach of promise. In the course of the proceedings, Mary was arrested three times—once for suborning perjury, once for threatening bodily harm, and once for embezzling money by refusing to pay $1.40 in witness fees to her client's mother. When a judge found her guilty of the latter charge, Mary refused to pay the $18 fine, so the judge tossed her into jail.

Several young friends convinced an appeals court to release Mary on a technicality, but she still could not restrain her tart tongue. "I think my release on a writ of habeas corpus saved my life, and maybe his [the judge's]," she blurted to a newspaper reporter. "Nobody knows what the result may be if such a misfortune happens to me again."

The Branson case dragged on, providing plenty of juicy headlines for the local newspapers. The jury finally ruled in favor of Wickstrom, a decision that infuriated Mary. She demanded a new trial. However, her client had had enough of her antics and publicly fired her.

Never one to slouch away from a slight, Mary announced in court that her former client and others had conspired to prevent her from getting her fee. She declared that she was now convinced the whole affair was an attempt to swindle Wickstrom. She withdrew her request for a new trial.

Any satisfaction that Mary might have gained from her vengeance was short-lived. Two days later, she was arrested on other charges related to the same case.

Another of Mary's conflicts with the courts began in late August 1897, when she was arrested for threatening the life of William Ballis, owner of a rooming house for local prostitutes. Mary claimed to have a personal relationship with Ballis and to share ownership of the building, but Ballis stoutly denied both claims. When he tried to evict her from the building, he said, she threatened him with a pistol. The resulting trial, according to the *Oregonian*, was "highly amusing at every stage, as it developed all the tribulations this lone female member of Oregon's bar has suffered for a long time past, and wrought havoc with many hopes entertained by different persons that the past was buried."

Mary admitted in court that she had wielded a gun, but it was too small, she said, to do much harm. The judge was not amused. He placed her under a $100 "peace bond" that he hoped would keep her under control—at least for the time being.

Mary chose to see this as a victory and planned a celebration. With characteristic immodesty, she issued a statement to the press in which she described herself as "not young or stylish withal she is comely and attractive, posessed [sic] of sparkling wit, and her company pleases young attorneys."

As the years passed, Mary grew even more eccentric. In late 1906 or early 1907, a middle-aged alcoholic named Anthony G. Ryan hired her to protest the appointment of a guardian who was to keep him from drinking away his assets. One of the key assets was a farm in the Powell Valley worth more than twenty thousand dollars. Mary arranged to have Ryan deed the farm to her. She said she would hold the farm in trust until she could get the guardianship dissolved. Then she would return to Ryan a half-interest in the farm and keep the other half as her fee.

Ryan agreed to the plan, even though he had no legal right to transfer the title without the approval of his court-appointed guardian. Mary began her attack on the guardianship arrangement with a volley of motions, petitions, briefs, and affidavits. She also began to worry that her fee might be in jeopardy because Ryan's health was failing—so she filed her own personal lawsuit to get title to the farm. Ryan's guardian countersued.

The case dragged on for years, in large part because Mary continually filed papers alleging all manner of conspiracies and improprieties. She generated "page after messy page of fustian fulmination, much of it incoherent, some of it illegible, and all of it done in her pitiful scrawl," according to historian Clark, who profiled Mary for the *Oregon Historical Quarterly* .

"Time had moved forward, Mary had not," he said in his 1955 article. "It was no longer possible to practice law by ear. The typewriter had come into general use, and the rules of court procedure had become more strict and particular."

The judge agreed with Mary's opponents that her legal brief was a mess. He ordered her to seek the help of another attorney to draft a proper brief, but the deadline for its submission came and went. When the judge dismissed Mary's case, she finally leaped into action. She asked other attorneys for help, but no one was willing to get involved in such an ill-fated case. Mary went back to writing her own briefs, charging that the judge had threatened her and showed favoritism for the plaintiff.

This allegation was too much for another judge who had since taken over the case. He dismissed it for good in June 1912. While Portland officials had once been amused by Mary's antics, they now considered her a crank and a nuisance.

No longer could Mary bluster her way through sticky situations. Nearly seventy years old, she was financially ruined and her law practice was in a shambles. Her health, too, was crumbling. She entered Multnomah County Hospital on October 11, 1912, and died thirteen days later of heart failure.

While Mary commanded little respect by the end of her career, she had become something of an Oregon legend. According to one bit of popular but far-fetched lore, a sea captain "shanghaied" her from an Italian port when she was sixteen and brought her to Portland, where he supposedly imprisoned her and treated her cruelly. One day, he was found murdered, and Mary was charged with the crime. She spoke no English, so she spent her time in jail learning the language and the law. She was such a quick study that she assisted in her own defense and was acquitted.

This melodramatic story could have been the script for one of the silent films of the early 1900s. Mary would likely have loved it. In fact, she probably would have insisted on playing the starring role. But Mary Leonard needed no movie to immortalize her life. Even without embellishment, it was as dramatic and entertaining as any film could be. ⚜

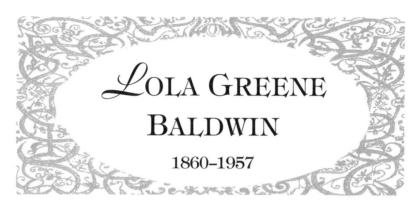

LOLA GREENE BALDWIN
1860–1957

Premier Policewoman

Lola Baldwin surveyed the small, dingy room in the Portland lodging house with horror. Its only furnishings were a rickety chair and a flimsy, narrow bed. On that bed lay the bodies of two destitute young women who, in Lola's words, had "chosen a death by suicide rather than a life of discouragement, misery, and sin." The girls' meager possessions were stashed in a pair of baking-powder tins. In their closet hung several cheap dresses and "crepe paper gew-gaws" they had worn to local dance halls in the evenings.

This was just the sort of grisly incident that had prompted the Portland police department to hire Lola in 1908—a move that gave her the distinction of being the first policewoman in the nation. Her job was to protect the moral welfare of young women and girls, and for the next dozen years she would do so with exceptional zeal and skill.

Lola envisioned her job as much more than cracking down on female lawbreakers. She was one of the country's first proponents of preventive policing. In her opinion, government and social organizations had a responsibility to "weed out the evil environments that lead to crime" and, in particular, to steer vulnerable women

Lola Greene Baldwin

away from trouble. This maternal approach would earn her the nick-name "Municipal Mother."

In the course of her career, Lola would lobby for laws to protect women's health and welfare, hound state officials into opening a home for troubled women, advise other states and cities on women's law-enforcement issues, and crusade vigorously against vice and corruption. She also would prove through her own accomplishments that women could play a valuable role in law enforcement.

"Baldwin's true legacy survives in the thousands of women who have followed in her professional footsteps," according to Gloria E. Myers, who wrote a comprehensive biography of Lola entitled *A Municipal Mother*. "Although Baldwin herself would probably have preferred that [female officers] remain 'separate but equal' [from male officers], the complete integration of women into modern law enforcement is a living monument to the efforts of Portland's pioneering female 'cop.'"

Prim and proper Lola certainly didn't seem destined for a job in law enforcement, although the foundation for her unusual career choice was laid early in life. Born in 1860 in Elmira, New York, she soon moved with her family to Rochester, where she attended the Christ Church Episcopal School for Girls. There, in addition to mastering reading, writing, and arithmetic, she absorbed the high moral standards needed to avoid life's "highways and resorts of dissipation."

When her father suddenly died in 1877, Lola had to quit high school and find a way to make a living. She taught school for several years in New York and Nebraska. Then, in 1884, she married LeGrand Baldwin, a Lincoln dry-goods merchant. Eventually, she quit working to stay home with their two sons.

Because she had been forced to venture out on her own at an early age, Lola empathized with young women struggling to make their way in the world. She began to do volunteer work to help "wayward" girls. When her husband took a job in Portland in 1904, Lola volunteered at the local Florence Crittenton Home, a refuge for young, unwed mothers.

Portland was scheduled to host the Lewis and Clark Centennial Exposition in 1905, and the city expected an influx of more than a million visitors. Unfortunately, some of them would be pickpockets, con men, and shysters, but there would also be legions of young women, lured to the city by its bright lights and the prospect of finding a temporary job at the fair. Concerned that some of these vulnerable young women might be led astray, members of the local Young Women's Christian Association decided to establish a Travelers' Aid program.

The notion that society should provide guidance and protection for young women was a product of the Progressive movement that was sweeping the nation. Women's roles were being redefined. Many women believed that, in addition to their duties at home, they had a responsibility to help cure the ills of urban America. This conviction had led to a burgeoning "social hygiene" movement that aimed to make cities safer, both morally and physically, for families, children, and working single women. Reformers sought to improve public-health programs, aid impoverished immigrants, ensure education for all children, and combat vice. As this reform effort gathered steam, America was shaking off the shackles of the Victorian Age and entering a "ragtime" era of more relaxed social morés.

Lola marched in the front lines of the social hygiene reformers, and her volunteer work so impressed YWCA officials that they offered her seventy-five dollars a month to run their Travelers' Aid program. Lola leaped at the chance to protect young women from moral pitfalls. In her new role, she helped newcomers find safe housing, checked out job offerings, arranged free medical care and temporary shelter, and exposed massage parlors that were really fronts for brothels.

Lola and her workers helped more than 1,500 young women and girls during the exposition. Writing in *Sunset* magazine in 1912, Louise Bryant attributed Lola's success to

> the fact that she is on good terms with the girls with whom she deals. She is a Big Mother to them all. She develops in them a sense of companionship that invites their confidence. In a tawdry, foolish, self-conscious girl she sees qualities upon which to build for her future as a good citizen and perhaps a mother.

The case of an unwed and impoverished pregnant girl named Caroline was typical of the lengths to which Lola would go to help her charges. She arranged to get food, baby clothes, and shelter from various charities and found a doctor willing to examine the girl for free. The doctor discovered that Caroline had tuberculosis and would need a cesarean section.

Undaunted, Lola persuaded Good Samaritan Hospital to admit Caroline free of charge. Then she marched the girl to the district attorney's office and demanded that officials press charges against the irresponsible father. After the baby's birth, Lola persuaded the Florence Crittenton Home to shelter the young mother and child. And when Caroline developed medical complications, Lola made sure she was treated at the county hospital. Lola even found the girl a job and arranged child care for the infant.

Lola was shrewd enough to recognize the public-relations value of cases such as Caroline's. She kept meticulous records and, from them, compiled disturbing statistics. She alerted the press to an increase in vice in the city and pointed out that most of the victims were local girls and women, not outsiders.

The problems actually multiplied after the closure of the fair.

As the temporary jobs disappeared, many young women could find no suitable employment. Desperate as they were, they were easy prey for procurers.

Lola's findings alarmed city officials, particularly Mayor Harry Lane, a physician who had made a campaign promise to curtail vice, promote public health, and make Portland "America's healthiest city." Lola had little trouble convincing him that he should add a woman to the city's police force in order to combat vice crimes involving women. Lola applied for the new job, got a high score on the civil-service exam, and was hired at the age of forty-eight.

Lola performed her new job from her old office at the YWCA. She argued that troubled women wouldn't seek help if they had to visit the station house. Her monthly salary was $150—about $35 more than most male detectives made—but she quelled any criticism by noting that her position required special training and that she had accomplished more in her three years with the YWCA than a dozen regular patrolmen could possibly have done.

In her first monthly report to the police chief, Lola hinted at her novel approach to police work. Rather than tout arrests and investigations, she noted that her "chief aim and purpose was to *prevent* downfall and crime among women and girls by investigation, timely aid, and admonition." This emphasis on preventive policing would become a hallmark of her career.

Lola believed that young women who moved to Portland to find work were particularly susceptible to temptation and exploitation. She estimated there were ten thousand such women in the city.

"The average working girl is lamentably ignorant and innocent of the ways of the tempter, whether he appears clothed in a dress suit or rough homespun," she once said.

Often, other police officers and health workers brought such girls to Lola's attention. She would find them jobs or places to live, enroll them in job-training courses, and help them deal with abusive bosses or customers.

When fortune-tellers in Portland began using attractive girls to lure customers, Lola led a movement to run the fortune-tellers out of town. She also targeted massage parlors, shooting galleries, dance halls, and saloons—any business that exploited pretty young women.

Once, Lola sent an investigator to several of the more notorious shooting galleries. He reported that female employees were performing "can-can" dances, hugging and kissing drunken men, and otherwise acting in a "disreputable manner." These shooting galleries, he believed, were "mere blinds for houses of prostitution."

Lola confirmed his suspicion with her own investigation. Armed with her findings, she pressured city officials to stop amusement businesses from hiring young women and dooming them "inexorably to moral ruin."

Next, Lola targeted the local dance halls, which were scandalizing Portland by offering jazz and ragtime music and featuring sexually suggestive dances. She discovered that innocent girls were being plied with liquor and thrust into the arms of lecherous men. "The great majority of women and girls owe their downfall to the dance hall," she declared.

She campaigned for a crackdown on these places of "unmitigated evil" and was a key proponent of a plan to license and inspect them. She also wanted to prevent them from serving liquor, to ban dancing on Sundays, and to prohibit unseemly dance steps. With a few modifications, the city adopted the new restrictions in 1913.

As the cultural climate of the nation evolved in the early 1900s, so did Lola's targets. She spoke out against vaudeville acts, movies, literature, and even clothing that she considered too racy. Her attempts at censorship may seem oppressive today, but at the time there was strong sentiment for policing morality.

Likewise, many Portland residents backed Lola's efforts to crack down on abortion practitioners. She used decoys to gather evidence and then prosecuted abortionists, and she campaigned against newspaper ads that touted abortion or birth control.

Lola also took aim against venereal disease, pulling into custody infected young women and requiring them to get treatment. She arrested young women who wore men's clothing and were thought to be lesbians, and she led raids that she hoped would shut down Portland's sex trade.

Although Lola was aggressive in her pursuit of unmarried mothers and the men who impregnated them, she didn't consider jail the best solution to the problem. Instead, she arranged social services for single mothers and insisted that they reveal the identities of the delinquent fathers. Many men decided it was more prudent to marry than to face prosecution for seduction.

Lola believed that crime-prevention programs were at least as important as corrective measures. "A fence around the top of the cliff is better than an ambulance down in the valley," she once said. One of her strategies was to persuade city officials to banish women from saloons. Another was to establish an after-care program that monitored delinquent girls to make sure they stayed out of further trouble. Still another was to lobby for creation of a state home for delinquent girls. The Oregon legislature approved funding for such a home in 1913. It became known as Hillcrest.

Word spread of Lola's aggressive and progressive programs to curb vice. She began to travel around the country to explain her tactics, and in 1917 she was appointed regional field secretary of the national Committee on Protective Work for Women and Girls. The goal of the committee was to police prostitutes infected with venereal diseases so that they would not threaten the health of World War I troops headed for Europe. Lola supervised the development of "war emergency" moral standards, as well as venereal disease treatment and prevention services in the Northwest. A year later she was promoted to oversee the program for the entire Pacific Coast and Arizona.

True to form, Lola was a zealous pursuer of her cause. She had strong public support because of the widespread fear that prostitution was exposing soldiers to serious health risks. Few people cared about the concern of some civil libertarians that Lola's program violated the rights of innocent women.

Lola considered her wartime job the highlight of her career, but it soon ended. In 1920, at age sixty, Lola returned to her old post with the city of Portland. She recognized that times had changed and her influence was waning, so she retired from the police force on May 1, 1922. After seventeen years of influencing local, regional, and national women's safety, she was tired of fighting the good fight. According to author Myers:

> Her writings at the time of her retirement indicate a certain weariness of spirit which seemed compounded by societal changes around her. She appeared to have a difficult time readjusting to postwar civilian duty once she shed her federal authority. As if her years of vigilance had had no effect whatever, the "Ragtime Era" had slipped unhindered into the "Jazz Age." The removal of wartime restrictions bared a Portland with drastically transformed social and cultural mores.

Even in retirement, Lola resisted societal changes of which she didn't approve. She complained bitterly of the "new woman" who smoked cigarettes, drank liquor, and otherwise "carried on." She wrote letters to newspapers and worked with women's groups, remaining active until her death in Portland on June 22, 1957.

While Lola often bemoaned changes that she thought would prove harmful to women, she herself was part of a major shift in the attitude of society toward the role of women. With energy and compassion, she had demonstrated that women were capable of working in a profession traditionally limited to men. Biographer Myers put it this way:

> [H]er strength of character, insistence on relative employment equality, and strict standards of investigation and professional behavior reserve an honored place for her in both law enforcement and women's history.... Portland's "Municipal Mother" ... should be remembered with genuine respect, and given her due as the nation's premier policewoman. ⚜

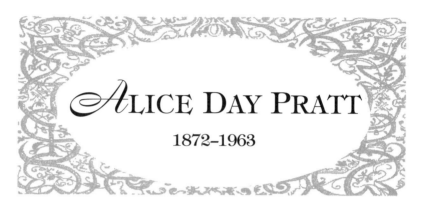

ALICE DAY PRATT
1872–1963

Dry-land Homesteader

$\mathcal{A}$lice Day Pratt shivered inside her canvas tent as the slate-gray sky spit snowflakes the size of dimes. For more than a month, temperatures had hovered near zero at her marginal homestead in central Oregon. Her supply of firewood was perilously low, and she could hardly find even slivers of juniper under the deepening snow.

Desperate for warmth, Alice split into kindling her large chopping block, the last relic of a wagonload of firewood that friends had delivered several months ago. It flared into a welcome blaze, but the comforting heat didn't last long.

Years later, she recalled her growing desperation as she struggled to survive single-handedly: "On the next day—the blizzard continuing—I burned my ladder, and on the next would have sacrificed my steps, had not a blessed chinook blown up in the night, carried the snow away in foaming torrents, and laid bare many a rich and unsuspected treasure of fuel."

The serendipitous chinook wind helped Alice to endure that grueling winter of 1913, but at least as significant were her own hard work, grit, and resourcefulness. She summoned those traits

Alice Day Pratt

time and time again as she tried to tame an unforgiving land, or at least to reach some kind of compromise with it. Although she eventually had to abandon her "homesteading dream," she managed to outlast many a fellow dreamer.

Later in life, Alice looked back on her homestead years with mixed feelings:

> I have known lean years and leaner years, hope and discouragement, good fortune and disaster, friendship and malice, righteousness, generosity, and double dealing. … Now and then I have known burdens—most often physical burdens—too heavy for mortals to bear. I have been cold and hungry and ragged and penniless. I have been free and strong and buoyant and glad.

Alice Day Pratt was part of the last wave of homesteaders who flooded the West in the early twentieth century—spurred on by passage of the Enlarged Homestead Act of 1909. Earlier emigrants to Oregon had already snatched most of the moist and fertile acreage in the western part of the state, so the latecomers had to settle for vast expanses of semiarid uplands east of the Cascades.

The new homesteaders often were unaware of how unforgiving and unprofitable this dry land could be. Pamphlets published by the railroads and other promoters had convinced them that the land was fecund and plentiful, just waiting to reward with riches those who got there first. The homesteaders also believed that the West offered adventure and independence. Here was one last chance to grab a piece of the quintessential American dream.

Alice herself had imagined being "afar on the prairies with the wind in my hair and the smell of new-plowed earth in every breath I drew." By heading west, she expected to put behind her a life of competition, high pressure, and "extremes of gayety [sic] and misery." Ahead, she envisioned hope, freedom, opportunity, and limitless spaces.

While Alice shared the same dreams and hopes of many homesteaders, she differed from most of them in an obvious way: She was a single woman in what was predominantly a man's world. Of the tens of thousands of people who filed homestead claims in the early 1900s, only about ten to fifteen percent were unmarried women, according to some historians.

Alice was unique in yet another way. She was one of only a few women who left behind an extensive firsthand account of her homesteading experience. In her book *A Homesteader's Portfolio*, published in 1922, she described how she moved to Oregon at the age of thirty-nine and "proved up" a homestead some sixty miles east of Bend. In engaging detail, she told of enduring drought and dust, hostile neighbors and hungry hawks, loneliness and larcenous rabbits. Although she presented the book as a work of fiction, the account is obviously autobiographical.

Author Molly Glass, in her introduction to the book, described it as "an especially significant work" because it presented "not only a rare but an extraordinarily complete report of the life of a single-handed woman homesteader on a landscape fraught with peril and difficulty—a woman not the victim of her circumstances but taking her place as a part of history, and a maker of history."

Over the years, Alice wrote other articles and books, including a self-published memoir, *Three Frontiers*, which delved into her Minnesota childhood. She was born in June 1872 to William and Sophie Pratt at the family's cottage near Mankato. Her father, a native of Connecticut, thrived on adventure but wasn't particularly adept at business. When his lumber company began to fail in 1877, he set off for the Black Hills of South Dakota, hoping to establish a prosperous lumber business among the hordes of miners lured there by

CROOK COUNTY HISTORICAL SOCIETY, BOWMAN MUSEUM

Alice Day Pratt

the discovery of gold. He left his young family behind and returned home only for brief visits. Not until 1886 was the family reunited on a remote homestead in Little Elk Canyon, fifteen miles north of Rapid City and twenty-five miles from William Pratt's business in Deadwood.

Alice's father continued to spend much of his time away from home, so many of the heavy chores fell to her. She helped care for two younger siblings and an ailing grandfather, toted heavy pails of water up a steep slope from a spring, tended the garden, looked after the horses, and trekked two miles to a small country store when the family needed supplies.

Alice's only schooling took place at home. She pored over books about plants and animals and hiked the Black Hills collecting specimens for her studies. Her interest in natural history became a lifelong pursuit. She wrote essays about flora and fauna for various magazines, and she published a children's book, *Animal Babies,* in 1941.

Although Alice's childhood in South Dakota was stark and demanding, she later would remember those years fondly. "We were always warm in the house and no fears beset us," she wrote. "Life was so simple that not much could happen to it."

Eventually, Alice left home to become a teacher. But, after working at schools in North Carolina and Arkansas, she pined for a more adventurous life. She began thinking seriously about her childhood desire to acquire her own "portion of the earth's crust" on the Western frontier. She had very little money and couldn't afford to buy land, but she knew she could get some free if she homesteaded. She decided to take a teaching job in northeastern Oregon where she could begin scouting for promising property.

Once in Oregon, Alice hired a "locator," who identified 160 acres in the middle of the state, near a tiny town called Post. As soon as Alice heard about the parcel in the fall of 1911, she dashed off to inspect it. She was smitten at first sight. Standing at the foot of Friar Butte amid sagebrush and junipers, she envisioned the butte as her upland pasture. The deep wash at its foot she saw planted in grain. Off in the distance, she spotted timbered mountains and a cleft cut by the Crooked River. She could see no houses or other signs of human habitation.

Alice knew she was home. She selected a handsome, cone-shaped juniper and decided it would stand in her dooryard. As she turned and looked over the sweeping valley, she picked a name for her homestead: Broadview.

Alice's first order of business was to file the proper papers at the local land office. Under the Enlarged Homestead Act, she got title to the land, but she couldn't sell or mortgage it until she had lived there and made improvements for three years.

Her second order of business was to return to northeastern Oregon to complete the school year and pack her belongings. She arrived back at her dry-land homestead on June 20, 1912, pitched a tent, and set to work. Homestead law required her to cultivate five of every forty acres within three years of taking possession. She had equipment to assemble, fields to plow, seed to buy, shelters to erect, firewood to collect, water to haul—so many chores they were nearly overwhelming.

Alice realized she would need help. When some of her new neighbors stopped by to say hello, she asked about the availability of hired hands. A few of the neighbors volunteered assistance, but rarely did they commit to a specific task and time. Once, neighbors offered to haul wood to help her construct a tent house, but they postponed the job week after week, even as fall approached.

Early one August, another neighbor agreed to plow forty acres so Alice could plant a wheat crop, but by mid-October the sod still lay undisturbed. Finally, the ground froze so hard it would no longer yield to the plow. An irate Alice later learned that the man had taken other jobs and had been leaving hers for last. As a result, she would have no wheat crop the following spring.

"My difficulties have been far oftener with the human element than with the rigors of the climate or the hardships of labor," she wrote in *A Homesteader's Portfolio*.

Alice had most of her problems with "Old Oregonians"— longtime ranchers who disdained the new homesteaders. One of them once bluntly told her, "The only way to deal with them home-steaders is to starve 'em out."

Fortunately, Alice also had a handful of good, caring, helpful friends, most of them newly arrived homesteaders like herself. With them, she enjoyed basket socials, dances, picnics, pageants, and other pleasant gatherings. These were welcome diversions from the physical and psychological hardships of her life.

Being a single woman, Alice occasionally found herself deflecting the advances of local bachelors. She feared "the life-long bond" of marriage, but, to her own surprise, she found some men appealing. After an evening walk with one young friend and neighbor, she confessed, "What sort of old maid am I anyway that I can't walk home in the moonlight with an attractive boy without tingling from head to foot! Good reason why devoted hermits segregate themselves. In the peace of Broadview I haven't felt this way for lo these many moons."

With few friends and neighbors on whom she could rely, Alice often turned to animal companions to help her combat the loneliness of her solitary life. She kept cats, horses, dogs, and chickens. The latter, she wrote, would "gather in little groups about me as I work here and there, engaging me in cheery conversation, essaying little familiarities and friendly overtures, even performing certain stunts with self-conscious gravity, delighting in personal attention."

Alice also felt a special attachment to her milk cow, Bossy, and Bossy's calf, Psalmmy. The calf resisted Alice's efforts to wean it, but she badly needed Bossy's milk for her own consumption and to earn extra income. When Alice confined Bossy to pasture, Psalmmy would follow Alice around the yard, suck the doorknob of her house, and roll his eyes to express his hunger. The calf was clever enough to circumvent Alice's many creative attempts to restrain him. When she tried muzzles, Psalmmy simply nuzzled them aside. When she smeared red-pepper paste on Bossy's teats, Psalmmy smacked his lips but then ignored the fiery sauce. When Alice built a fence to corral Bossy, Psalmmy found a gap. Years later, Alice described her frustrations.

I tried another fence. I tried another pasture. I tried the government reserve twenty miles distant. Always sundown of a day sooner or later arrived that brought Bossy and Psalmmy peacefully home together, Bossy released of her rich and ample load, Psalmmy rolling in his gait and stupid to inebriety. No wires were too closely set, no gate too high, no location too distant for the ingenuity or the valor of his ruling passion.

Neighbors counseled Alice to butcher Psalmmy, but she couldn't do it; she had become too attached to the clever calf. Instead, she finally erected a fence tall enough to complete the job of weaning.

Domestic critters were not Alice's only worries. She battled coyotes that harassed her stock, rabbits that munched her crops, and hawks that snatched her chickens. She scared away some of the hawks with well-timed shotgun blasts but failed to hit any. She tried poisoning the rabbits but had limited success.

In truth, Alice did not have the heart to try more lethal weapons. In her writings, she lamented the cruelty that was needed to keep the pests under control. She also worried about upsetting the balance of nature—a decidedly progressive sentiment for an early-twentieth-century homesteader. She wrote:

For a thousand years, presumably, this vast plateau which is now my home has been covered with sagebrush and bunch grass and sprinkled with juniper trees, and has supported a normal population of jack rabbits and sage rats. Then suddenly comes man with his alien stock, his dogs and his cats, his new and succulent crops, with their admixture of weed seeds and germs of insect life. And lo, this quiet and harmonious state of nature is all in turmoil.

Alice's own existence on her dry-land homestead was always tenuous. She spent several years living in a tent house, which would shake "like a rat" in storms and heat up like an oven on blistering summer days. It was cozy in the winter only if she had plenty of firewood.

Eventually, neighbors helped her to build a barn and a rickety twenty-by-twelve-foot wooden house. It had a single room with a kitchen and shelves at one end and a table, cot, and bookshelves at the other.

Alice could not afford a sturdier home or more household conveniences. She had to horde her money for necessities, such as seeds and plowing. She sold chickens, eggs, alfalfa, hay, grain, and vegetables, but her earnings never amounted to much. At times, she had to take teaching jobs to make ends meet.

As soon as Alice proved up her homestead by meeting the residency requirement, she traveled to the East to visit her family and earn some money. She returned to Broadview two years later, in 1918, but funds were still short and she had to take another teaching job ten miles away at Conant Basin. It enabled her to cling to her "homesteading dream" despite the drought, bad weather, and poor commodity prices that had driven so many others off the land. In 1921, she wrote:

> Over my six hundred and forty acres—thus increased by a second beneficent allowance—roams a beautiful little Jersey herd. A group of dear white ponies call me mistress. White biddies still dot my hill slopes and cackle ceaselessly. Pax, an Armistice Day puppy, and El Dorado, son of Kitty Kat, have succeeded those earlier friends whose gentle spirits still wander with me on the sagebrush slopes. There is a mortgage. There is still necessity to teach. My little flock of orphan citizens still beckons

from the future. Yet, for me, the wilderness and the solitary place have been glad, and nature has not betrayed the heart that loved her.

Alice held onto her homestead even as drought persisted into the 1920s. The good topsoil blew away, wells dried up, and the soil grew more alkaline. To make things worse, prices for grain and dairy products were dropping, and harsh winters battered the plains. The winter of 1924–1925 was ruthless. One day a blinding storm dumped enough snow to reach the upper sashes of the school where Alice was teaching. Two days later, temperatures plummeted to thirty-three degrees below zero—the lowest Alice had ever experienced. She had to kick her way through deep snow to check on her chickens. As she later recalled:

> Twenty young cocks, as white as the snow drifts, sat starkly upon their perches as if enchanted. There was a statuesqueness about them that sent a chill over me, cold as I was. No, they were not dead, but thos [sic] wattles that characterize their breed were as hard and stiff as plaster. Their feet were not frozen. It was the evening dip in the water that had done the mischief. Dabbling in the water had started the freezing before the night's cold had found them. Full-feeding was all that had saved the flock from death.

On her way back to her house, Alice was struck by its appearance, "lost in the wilderness of snow, and fringed with icicles almost to the ground." Later in her life, as she lay in bed in a comfortably warm apartment, she sometimes wondered if the little house still stood "in a wilderness of snow, and whether little calves are crying in the willows."

After that frigid winter, Alice enjoyed a few years of better weather, but it was not to last. Another drought struck in 1928. Alice was forced to take out a large loan, and a year later she had to sell her dairy herd to repay it. In 1930, she gave her chickens and horses to neighbors, shuttered her little house on the prairie, and climbed on the train for one last trip to the East. She must have held out hope of seeing Broadview again, because she didn't sell it until 1950.

Most dry-land settlers had packed up and fled long before Alice. By 1920, only half of the original homestead population remained. By 1940, two-thirds of the land allotted under the homestead act had reverted to the federal government.

After moving back to the East, Alice lived with her mother and her sister Marjorie, first in Niagara Falls and then in New York City. She continued to teach and write magazine articles and books. Some of her manuscripts were published, while others gathered dust on a shelf. Late in life, Alice suffered from crippling arthritis and was confined to her apartment, though her intellect and spirit remained strong to the end. Alice died on January 11, 1963, at the age of ninety.

Although, in the long run, Alice had not succeeded at homesteading, she had demonstrated the stamina and resourcefulness of women at a time when women's capabilities were underestimated. She had also learned a valuable lesson, which she summed up shortly after turning eighty:

> Success may be the smallest and least important of the fruits of endeavor; it is the endeavor itself, the opportunity to use one's whole self completely—initiative, creativity, and physical strength—that is its own reward: and it may well be that one looks back upon the times of

greatest strain and anxiety as the high points in [one's] pilgrimage. ⚜

Hazel Hall
1886–1924

Fettered Poet

Hazel Hall sat at the second-story window of her Portland home, embroidering a piece of linen and listening for passersby. When at length she did hear the scuffle of feet outside, she reached eagerly for the hand mirror that she always kept beside her. Confined to a wheelchair since the age of twelve, she was unable to stand and watch the bustling world go by. So she held up the mirror at an angle, hoping to capture the image of the pedestrian below. Would she glimpse a salesman trudging home from a long day's work? A mother scurrying from the grocery store with the makings of a family dinner? A child skipping down the block in search of a playmate?

Hazel could only guess at the identity and destiny of each reflected passerby. It was a terrible handicap for someone who aspired to be a poet, to be so isolated from the human drama. Yet Hazel refused to abandon her dream. She mastered her disability by using the tools she had at hand: the mirror, the window—and her imagination. In one of her first published poems, "The Hand-Glass," she described life from her unique perspective:

Hazel Hall

I am holding up a mirror
To look at life: in my hand-glass
I see a strange, hushed street below me
Where people pass.
The street is coloured like a picture,
And people passing there
Move with the majesty of story,
And are less real and wise than fair.

Looking at life in a mirror
Is distortion. I must see
Through the paint the flimsy canvas,
I must be
Cynical, and judge no passer
By the colour of a dress—
O eyes that must learn from a mirror,
Search for dust and bitterness!

While poetry helped Hazel to cope with the boredom and frustrations of life as an invalid, it also brought her a measure of acclaim. Three volumes of her verse were published in the 1920s. Dozens of her poems appeared in anthologies and popular magazines of the day, including *Harper's*, *New Republic*, *Century*, and *Sunset*.

In 1921, the prestigious magazine *Poetry* presented Hazel with its Young Poets' Prize. A year earlier, the *Boston Transcript*, one of the most acclaimed poetry forums of the time, selected her piece "Three Girls" as one of the five best poems in the nation. *Transcript* editor William Stanley Braithwaite applauded her "outstanding vision," undaunted though fate had "encased [her] spirit in a shell."

Despite such plaudits, Hazel's talent went largely unrecognized in Oregon. Caged in the home she shared with her sister and widowed mother, she was like a "stranger in her own city," the *Oregonian* reported at her sudden death in 1924.

Who was this frail young woman with the dramatic eyes and the rhyme and rhythm burning in her soul? Hazel was born February 7, 1886, in St. Paul, Minnesota, to Montgomery and Mary Garland Hall. She had two sisters, Ruth and Lulie. When Hazel was still a toddler, the family moved to Portland, where her father managed the express division of the Northern Pacific Railroad.

Hazel romped like any child until the age of twelve. Then, suddenly, her legs refused to move. The reason for her paralysis isn't clear: It has been attributed both to a fall and to a bout with scarlet fever. Whatever its cause, it forced her to drop out of the fifth grade and retire to a wheelchair. She continued her education on her own by reading extensively.

Hazel's sister Ruth, a longtime Portland school librarian, once recalled that she had "never known a better educated person, in the richest sense of the word. [Hazel] browsed where she wanted to … and with a broad intuitive sense, she grasped facts quickly in their entirety."

Poets were among Hazel's favorite authors. She devoured the works of Edna St. Vincent Millay, Emily Dickinson, and Robert Frost. She began writing when she was about nine years old. A few years later, as an invalid, she started a periodical she called *The Star Journal* and served as its editor, sole contributor, publisher, printer, and binder. She remembered it fondly:

I folded sheets of foolscap, sewed them together and decorated the outside one with many gold stars for a cover, then proceeded to rule off the inside pages into columns and to fill them with minute calligraphy, purported to be stories, articles, verse and the like. My sole remuneration—and these tasks were rather arduous, as I was strapped flat to my bed at the time—came from my family, who were compelled to pay ten cents each for the privilege of perusal.

Knowing that her limited mobility and education would hurt her chances of employment, Hazel eventually began looking for ways to work at home. She had always enjoyed sewing, and she discovered that wealthy families were eager to buy her finely handcrafted items: embroidered bridal robes and linens, baby dresses, shirts, and christening gowns. As she stitched, she hovered near her window to watch the passersby and the changing of the seasons.

Hazel also began to spend more time writing poetry, but it wasn't until 1916, when she was thirty, that she saw her first poem published in the *Boston Transcript*. The following year, she reached a nationwide audience when her work appeared in *The Masses*, a radical monthly magazine devoted to art and politics.

Hazel preferred to write in metrical verse, but she did experiment with free verse for awhile. Whatever the form, she found that she wrote best about the limited world she knew best: needlework, the changing seasons, and passersby. One of her first poems, "Two Sewing," wove together two of those themes and echoed the steady rhythm of her needle when she sewed:

The wind is sewing with needles of rain.
With shining needles of rain
It stitches into the thin
Cloth of earth. In,
In, in, in.
Oh, the wind has often sewed with me.
One, two, three.

Spring must have fine things

To wear like other springs.
Of silken green the grass must be
Embroidered. *One and two and three.*
Then every crocus must be made
So subtly as to seem afraid
Of lifting colour from the ground;
And after crocuses the round
Heads of tulips, and all the fair
Intricate garb that Spring will wear.
The wind must sew with needles of rain,
Stitching into the thin
Cloth of earth, in,
In, in, in,
For all the springs of futurity.
One, two, three.

The poem, part of Hazel's "needlework" series, found a place in her first book, *Curtains*, which was published in 1921. Many of her verses relied on sewing as a metaphor, and many appealed particularly to women, such as these lines from a piece entitled "Light Sleep":

Women who sing themselves to sleep
Lie with the hands at rest,
Locked over them night-long as though to keep
Music against their breast.

Poet Louise Townsend Nicholl once described Hazel's verses as "women poems." "The consciousness of a man, in that unveiled contact with reality, would be a different thing," Nicholl said. "It is not any poet speaking—it is a woman poet, poet woman."

Hazel's second book, *Walkers,* published in 1923, explored in more depth the world—and the walkers—outside her window. Harriet Monroe, editor of *Poetry* magazine, maintained that there might never be another poet "so sensitive to the music and beat of walking, marching, dancing feet.

"The rhythm of long procession dins into her ears and steps on and out until it fills space and time," Monroe said. "Her imagination is possessed by this unending march along the roadways of the world, symbolic of longer marches through infinite reaches of the soul."

Hazel heard many stories in the parade of footsteps that passed her house. She detected a whisper of dreaminess in one trio of girls who regularly walked by. It inspired her award-winning poem "Three Girls":

Three school girls pass this way each day.
Two of them go in the fluttery way
Of girls, with all that girlhood buys:
But one goes with a dream in her eyes.

Two of them have the eyes of girls
Whose hair is learning scorn of curls,
But the eyes of one are like wide doors
Opening out on misted shores.

And they will go as they go today
On to the end of life's short way;
Two will have what living buys,
And one will have the dream in her eyes.

Two will die as many must,
and fitly dust will welcome dust;
But dust has nothing to do with one—
She dies as soon as her dream is done.

While many of the poems in *Walkers* reflect an understanding of the passion and pathos of life, at least one critic, Portland writer Walt Curtis, found the book "so patently Freudian, desirous of being able to move and walk, that it borders, at times, on self-parody."

Nonetheless, *Walkers* was well-received by the public and sold more copies than either of Hazel's other books. Perhaps readers were simply curious about what a wheelchair-bound poet could have to say about walking. She did ponder what it would be like to walk again, but she did not permit herself to wallow in self-pity. As always, she accepted her fate gracefully.

Hazel even argued that her handicap gave her a certain advantage as a poet: She perceived in silence what others overlooked as they rushed noisily through their daily lives.

Hazel's sister Ruth insisted that Hazel never dwelled on her inability to walk:

When anyone speaks of my sister as crippled, I always feel rebellious, because she gave the impression of such abundant health. She enjoyed living immensely—her days were never long enough for all the activities she wished to press into them. Except that she did not walk, she was in good health until about six weeks before her death. … Unconsciously, I find myself judging people by her measurements, contrasting their brittleness of mind with her splendor and being incredibly sorry for humanity and myself in the bargain.

Hazel spent a great deal of time alone with her thoughts while her sister and mother were working. She was not completely housebound. There is evidence that she visited a local bookstore and that she took a sightseeing tour of the Columbia River Gorge, but even she described herself as a "shut-in."

As if Hazel's paralysis were not burden enough, her eyesight also faltered as she grew older, forcing her to abandon the intricate needlework she so enjoyed. She shifted her energy and attention entirely to writing poetry, and, as her body grew weaker, her verse grew stronger. Her determination to improve was reflected in a conversation that she had one evening with Ruth. "I am seeing so far tonight that I am blinded by the space between me and the inevitable," she said.

Hazel fell ill in 1924, and she seemed to sense the footsteps of death approaching. Characteristically, she confronted her end in her poetry. A collection of these "death poems" was published posthumously in 1928 under the title *Cry of Time*. One of these final poems, "Here Comes the Thief," illustrated the serene and lyrical way she approached her subjects and the stoical way in which she viewed the inevitability of death:

> Here comes the thief
> Men nickname Time,
> Oh, hide you, leaf,
> And hide you, rhyme.
> Leaf, he would take you
> And leave you rust.
> Rhyme, he would flake you
> With spotted dust.
> Scurry to cover,
> Delicate maid
> And serious lover.

Girl, bind the braid
Of your burning hair;
He has an eye
For the lusciously fair
Who passes by.
O lover, hide—
Who comes to plunder
Has the crafty stride
Of unheard thunder.
Quick—lest he snatch,
In his grave need,
And sift and match,
Then sow like seed
Your love's sweet grief
On the backward air,
With the rhyme and the leaf
And the maiden's hair.

Portland critic Curtis found Hazel's final poems "dazzling."
He wrote in 1988 that "one would have to look to Walt Whitman
to find anything quite like them, but he is too optimistic! ... Hall
meets death calmly, lucidly—but without pleasure. Reading *Cry of
Time* is like drowning."

When Hazel died on May 11, 1924, she passed "quietly, without pain," her sister Ruth reported. She was thirty-eight years old.
The cause of death, like the cause of her paralysis, was never defi-
nitely determined. Doctors blamed heart failure.

As isolated as she was from the world, Hazel would likely have
been surprised by the reaction to her death. Many people had been
touched by her poetry. In 1939, friends and admirers joined forces
to create the book *A Tribute to Hazel Hall*.

"God dropped Hazel Hall like a sapphire into a still sea," wrote one of the contributors. "Her brief sweet life made ripples, outgoing, widening to eternity. And every poem that she wrote rode forth, like a Sir Galahad, upon those ripples, and urged them on and on to a spaceless, timeless destiny."

After a period of popularity, Hazel's poetry drifted into obscurity, but it has been rediscovered in recent years. Her work is included in a national feminist anthology entitled *No More Masks* and is used today in university courses. Writer Susan Mach wrote a play about Hazel's life called *Monograms* that has been staged twice in recent years by the Portland Repertory Theater. Hazel's family home at 106 NW 22nd Place has been added to the National Register of Historic Places. Adjacent to the house is a "poetry garden" and memorial to Hazel, created recently by the Oregon Cultural Heritage Commission.

This renewal of interest helps to keep alive Hazel's poetry, as well as her poignant and inspiring story. It seems a fitting memorial to one who, though her life was short, illuminated the world around her in a way few others have. More than anything, she was, like the title of one of the last poems she penned before her death, a "Maker of Songs":

Take strands of speech, faded and broken;
Tear them to pieces, word from word,
Then take the ravelled shreds and dye them
With meanings that were never heard.

Place them across the loom. Let wind-shapes
And sunlight come in at the door,
Or let the radiance of raining
Move in silver on the floor.

More Than Petticoats

And sit you quiet in the shadow
Before the subtly idle strands.
Silence, a cloak, will weigh your shoulder;
Silence, a sorrow, fill your hands.

Yet there shall come the stirring . . . Weaver,
Weave well and not with words alone;
Weave through the pattern every fragment
Of glittered breath that you have known. ❧

OPAL WHITELEY
1897–1992

Prodigy or Fraud?

$\mathcal{E}$llery Sedgwick was used to turning people away from his office in Boston. As editor of the prestigious literary magazine *Atlantic Monthly*, he saw plenty of amateur authors and uninspired prose. But there was something intriguing about the dark-haired, doe-eyed woman who presented herself on a late September afternoon in 1919—"something very young and eager and fluttering," he later recalled, "like a bird in a thicket."

The woman introduced herself as Opal Whiteley, a twenty-one-year-old nature lover who had grown up in the logging camps of Oregon. Timidly, she gave him the manuscript that she hoped he would agree to publish. Entitled *The Fairyland Around Us*, it was a fanciful tale of beasts and blossoms, butterflies and birds. It was an odd creation, as one writer later described it, "hurriedly written, poorly edited, pathetically disorganized and patched together, yet filled with a unique charm."

Sedgwick found little to tempt him in the work and tactfully rejected it. Then, touched by Opal's disappointment and naiveté, he asked her to tell him a little about herself. "You must have had an interesting life," he prompted. "You have lived much in the woods?"

Opal Whiteley

Encouraged by his interest, Opal began to recount a childhood that included frequent forays into the Oregon wildwoods. There, she would commune with "God's little creatures" and with the "fairies" of the wind and trees and water. Her memories were so vivid that Sedgwick was inspired to ask if she'd kept a diary. She had, she replied, tears welling in her eyes, but her younger sister had torn it to bits during a fit of childish temper.

"You loved it?" he asked.

"Yes, I told it everything."

"Then you kept the pieces."

Sedgwick had accurately judged the young woman's nature. Yes, she had kept the pieces. They were stored in boxes in Los Angeles, where she recently had been staying. Sedgwick knew instinctively that this was the work he wanted to publish. He persuaded her to send for her mangled journal, and in his autobiography, *The Happy Profession*, he described its condition when it arrived:

We telegraphed for [the pieces], and they came, crammed in a hatbox, hundreds, thousands, one might say half a million of them. Some few were large as a half-sheet of notepaper; more, scarce big enough to hold a letter of the alphabet. The paper was of all shades, sorts, and sizes: butchers' bags pressed and sliced in two, wrapping paper, the backs of envelopes—anything and everything that could hold writing. The early years of the diary are printed in letters so close that, when the sheets are fitted, not another letter can be squeezed in. In later passages the characters are written with childish clumsiness, and later still one sees the gradually forming adult hand.

Sedgwick installed Opal in the home of his mother, and for the next nine months, the young woman laboriously pieced together the story of her girlhood—a story that within a year would make literary history. Each page of the diary was like a jigsaw puzzle, with every scrap frugally lettered on both sides. The fact that the writer had used a variety of colored crayons, one at a time until each was gone, helped to make the task a little easier.

In March 1920, *The Atlantic Monthly* began publishing in serial form the first two years of the diary—written, Opal said, when she was six and seven years old. It was an imaginative and ingenuous document, a view of nature through the eyes of a child. Its appeal lay in its poetic and perceptive insight into even the most mundane features of Opal's life. For example, when one day she had to pick potatoes, she described her humble harvest like this:

Potatoes are very interesting folks. I think they must see a lot of what is going on in the earth—they have so many eyes.... I did count the eyes that every potato did have, and their numbers were in blessings....

And all the times I was picking up potatoes, I did have conversations with them. Too, I did have thinks of all their growing days there in the ground, and all the things they did hear. Earth-voices are glad voices, and earth-songs come up from the ground through the plants; and in their flowering, and in the days before these days are come, they do tell the earth-songs to the wind. And the wind in her goings does whisper them to folks to print for other folks, so other folks do have knowing of earth's songs. When I grow up, I am going to write for children—and grownups that haven't grown up too much—all the earth-songs I now do hear.

In another passage, Opal was able to find pleasure even in a plague of wasps:

Sometimes I share my bread and jam with Yellowjackets, who have a home on the bush by the road, twenty trees and one distant from the garden. To-day I climbed upon the old rail fence close to their home with a piece and a half of bread and jam and the half piece for them and the piece for myself. But they all wanted to be served at once, so it became necessary to turn over all bread and jam on hand. I broke it into little pieces, and they had a royal feast there on the fence rail. I wanted my bread and jam; but then Yellowjackets are such interesting fairies, being among the world's first paper makers; and baby Yellowjackets are such chubby youngsters. Thinking of these things makes it a joy to share one's bread with these wasp fairies.

The journal also chronicled the daily adventures of Opal and her menagerie of pets, all of which bore weighty names that implied an amazing familiarity with the classics. There were Brave Horatius, the dog; Thomas Chatterton Jupiter Zeus, a "most dear velvety woodrat"; and Lars Porsena of Clusium, a pet crow "with a fondness for collecting things." Opal even christened some of the local flora. She gave the name Charlemagne to "the most tall tree of all the trees growing in the lane."

Sometimes, inexplicably, Opal lapsed into French to remark on *les fleurs* and *les riviéres*. Often, she referred to herself in her journal as *"petite Françoise."* It seemed a harmless fancy, but it was a hint of the tempest to come.

In a world wearied by war, Opal's diary was a refreshing

reminder of the beauty of God's earth and the innocence of a child's soul. Reaction to it was so positive that in September 1920 the Atlantic Monthly Press released it as a book entitled *The Story of Opal: The Journal of an Understanding Heart.*

It was an immediate bestseller on both sides of the Atlantic. The diary, gushed *The Christian Science Monitor*, showed "an intimacy with the ways of the trees and animals that makes her one of a company where Wordsworth and Hudson and Fabre were with her, loving the universe about them, quite unhemmed in by man's caste-conscious separation from it."

The *London Outlook* was equally impressed:

Quite frankly if we had not the author's word to the contrary, we should regard the publication in its tingling beauty of expression and amazing mastery of words as entirely beyond the powers of any small child of six. That any baby of that age, although she enjoys a communion with Nature in its most Wordsworthian sense, should have been able to achieve anything so constructive and consecutive seems to us little short of a miracle. It *is* a miracle, in fact. But so much admitted, little Opal Whiteley's diary provides us with a rich feast.

In Oregon, Opal's journal became one of the biggest news stories ever to break in the state. Newspapers devoted dozens if not hundreds of column inches to it each day. Some celebrated the diary as the work of a rare child prodigy, but skeptics in Oregon and elsewhere began to wonder whether it was too good to be true. Could it be a hoax, written by Opal in adulthood or by someone else entirely?

Nowhere was the diary more controversial than in Cottage Grove, Oregon, home of the Whiteley family. There, it was Opal's introduction to the book that really set tongues wagging, because in it she claimed that the Whiteleys were not her biological parents. She described an idyllic life with "angel" parents who took her on frequent nature walks until, tragically, they died.

No children I knew. There were only Mother and the kind woman who taught me and looked after me and dressed me, and the young girl who fed me. And there was Father, in those few days when he was home from the far lands. Those were wonderful days, his home-coming days. Then he would take me on his knee, and ride me on his shoulder, and tell me of the animals and birds of the far lands. And we went for many walks, and he would talk to me about the things along the way....

There was one day when I went with Mother in a boat. It was a little way on the sea. It was a happy day. Then something happened, and we were all in the water. Afterward, when I called for Mother, they said the sea waves had taken her, and she was gone to heaven. I remember the day because I never saw my mother again.

The time was not long after that day with Mother in the boat, when one day the kind woman who taught me and took care of me did tell me gently that Father too had gone to heaven, while he was away in the far lands. She said she was going to take me to my grandmother and grandfather, the mother and father of my father.

Opal also described embarking on a long journey with "strange people" who took her not to her grandparents but to Mrs. Whiteley.

The day they put me with her was a rainy day, and I thought she was a little afraid of them, too. She took me on the train and in a stage-coach to the lumber camp. She called me Opal Whiteley, the same name as that of another little girl who was the same size as I was when her mother lost her. She took me into the camp as her own child, and so called me as we lived in the different lumber camps and in the mill town.

In the introduction to her diary, Opal claimed to have no knowledge of the identity of her "real" parents. But months after the journal was published, an inquisitive reader found a tantalizing clue. Throughout the journal, Opal had included—for no apparent reason—several seemingly innocent lists of rivers and flowers and birds, all of them in French, though she claimed not to know the language. On one page, for example, she wrote, "I did sing the *riviére* a song. I sang it Le chant de Seine, de Havre, et Essonne et Nonette et Roullon et Iton et Darnetal et Ourcq et Rille et Loing et Eure et Audelle et Nonette et Sarc."

A reader studying this particular passage discovered that the first letters of the names, when placed together, spelled "Henri d'Orléans." This and other similar acrostics sprinkled throughout the diary seemed to suggest that Opal's angel father was none other than Henry, Duke of Orléans, a naturalist and great-grandson of the last king of France. In 1901, when Opal would have been almost four, Orléans had died during an expedition through India and Indochina. He had never married, but one writer has theorized that Opal was an illegitimate child he wanted to hide from enemies of the French monarchy.

Opal's relatives in Oregon vehemently denied her claim of foster parentage, and skeptics began to pick holes in her story. How could a child of five who had grown up in a French household speak perfect, unaccented English when she arrived in Oregon? How could this child resemble the Whiteleys so remarkably? How could friends and other relatives fail to notice the substitution of Opal for the Whiteley's missing child? How could Opal know details of the Whiteleys' early family life, such as the name of a dog they had owned when she was a toddler? How could she remember trivial events from her life with her angel parents at age three, yet not remember her "real" name?

Opal's fantastic tale of foster parentage dealt her diary a fatal blow. Readers who had been inclined to believe in the journal's authenticity began to speculate that if the angel-parent story were untrue, the rest of the diary was probably a fraud, as well. A year after *The Story of Opal* was published, it was allowed to slip quietly out of print. Opal left Boston for New York, moved on to Washington, D.C., and then, in 1923, fled to England.

Regardless of whether Opal was of royal heritage, she was unquestionably remarkable. As one biographer later observed, she was either "amazingly precocious at six and seven or amazingly imaginative and ingenious at nineteen and twenty."

Opal was born, according to the Whiteleys, on December 11, 1897, in Colton, Washington. The family moved to Oregon not quite five years later. Relatives later recalled that Opal could read by age three and was "always writing." Acquaintances said that she had the vocabulary of an adult by the time she was six.

Even as a child, Opal showed a special interest in science and nature. Elbert Bede, editor of the Cottage Grove newspaper and eventually author of an Opal biography, heard her give a forty-five-minute lecture illustrated with two rooms full of butterfly and rock specimens when she was only thirteen or fourteen years old. "She had an amazing knowledge of such things," Bede wrote later, "certainly a knowledge far beyond one of her years."

In 1915, while visiting an aunt in Eugene, Opal decided to

inspect the natural-history collections at the University of Oregon. She made a tremendous impression on the faculty, as well as on the local media. "She knows more about geology than do many students that have graduated from my department," a geology professor told the Eugene *Daily Guard*. "She may become one of the greatest minds Oregon has ever produced."

"I never saw anyone so hungry for knowledge," another professor raved. "She just eats it up like a person starved."

The following year, Opal enrolled as a freshman at the university, paying for her education at least in part by traveling throughout the state giving lectures on nature. Halfway through her second year, her money ran out, so she flitted to southern California, hoping to find a part in the movies. When after six weeks she had failed to impress a single Hollywood director, she resorted again to lecturing and teaching. One series of talks, entitled "The Fairyland Around Us," was particularly successful. Opal decided to incorporate them into a book.

For three exhausting months, Opal worked on the first draft of *The Fairyland Around Us*, sometimes writing for as many as twelve to sixteen hours a day. Meanwhile, to pay for the book's publication, she began soliciting advance orders from some of the most affluent and influential people in the nation, including John D. Rockefeller and Andrew Carnegie. Her audacity helped earn her more than $9,000, but as publication progressed she made so many editing changes that the cost of printing exceeded her means. When she was unable to pay the extra expenses, the printer refused to finish the job and destroyed the plates.

Opal was devastated and for a time had to be hospitalized. Friends urged her to take her book to the East Coast and seek a publisher there. So, in the summer of 1919, she borrowed money for the trip to Boston and her fateful meeting with Ellery Sedgwick.

At least two writers who have researched Opal's life believe she wrote or revised her diary during her stay in Los Angeles, when she was about twenty years old. Inez Fortt, a former librarian at the University of Oregon, came to this conclusion at least in part because of the testimony of a woman with whom Opal lived in California, Maude Harwood Bales.

"Opal spent her days and most of her evenings in her upstairs room where she closeted herself for long hours of writing," Fortt quoted Bales as saying. One day, Bales walked past Opal's open bedroom door and noticed large sheets of paper spread out on the bed. Each was crowded with printed letters at least an inch high—much like those in the diary Opal would soon reconstruct for Sedgwick.

Opal made ample use of Bales's personal library, which included many of the classics and a volume called *French Self-Taught*. She also spent entire days at the city library thumbing through travel and history books, as well as several obscure volumes written by Henri d'Orléans about his travels.

"Could this have been the time Opal was writing her 'six-year-old' diary?" Fortt speculated in a 1969 article for *Old Oregon* magazine. She went on to answer her own question:

> Everything I have learned about Opal in the last two decades points in this direction. Confused and defeated [because of the failure of *The Fairyland Around Us*], dependent on the generosity of friends and acquaintances, Opal probably withdrew from life about her. Only in her room was she able to "lose" herself and forget the present. There she could relive a dream of the past, her childhood in the woods with the little animals who accompanied her on explorations, and where she had been a Princess in a Fairyland. And as she regressed in her mind to the past, she thought as a child and wrote as a child. She was no longer

Opal Whiteley but a royal Princess. As she sat and printed, the dream and the reality fused together, and the child-princess and Opal became one.

Elbert Bede, who wrote *Fabulous Opal Whiteley* in 1954, came to a more skeptical conclusion. While he thought Opal's published diary did represent in part a journal she had kept as a child, he believed she substantially embellished it during her stay in Los Angeles—with the help of "an older intellectual adult." After noting that some passages from *The Fairyland Around Us* appear almost verbatim in *The Story of Opal*, he went on to suggest that

> someone had to spend a great amount of time searching in scarce biographies and other somber tomes not readily available in public libraries. To assume the two books were written concurrently or consecutively places their production during the eighteen months Opal lived in California. . . . Her seemingly almost super-human efforts during that year and a half in editing and publishing *The Fairyland Around Us* . . . [were] more than enough to take all the available time and energy of one person, even one as energetic and as indomitable as Opal. . . .
>
> The improvements in *The Story of Opal* suggest rather convincingly that an associate joined with Opal in producing a sensational manuscript, with *The Fairyland Around Us* as the skeleton.

Bede even claimed to know the name of Opal's collaborator, but he refused to reveal it in his book, because, he said, he was unable to prove it.

Although it's easy to dismiss *The Story of Opal* as an elaborate and calculated hoax, there are those who wholeheartedly embrace it as the work of a child prodigy. Sedgwick of the *Atlantic Monthly* was one of these. He remained "utterly convinced" of the "rightness and honesty of the manuscript as the *Atlantic* printed it."

Another believer is Benjamin Hoff, best known as author of *The Tao of Pooh*. After discovering an old, worn copy of the diary on a shelf of a Portland public library in 1983, he took it home, read it, and was enchanted by its "haunting, time-arresting" quality. He set out to discover why it was not an American classic.

Drawing on previous experience as an investigative reporter, Hoff interviewed every friend, relative, teacher, classmate, and acquaintance of Opal he could find—including one childhood chum who said she had seen the torn pages of the diary not long after a tearful Opal had collected all the pieces. What Hoff learned led him to conclude that *The Story of Opal* was the work of a budding genius no less remarkable than Wolfgang Amadeus Mozart, who, after all, had begun composing music at the age of six. Of the diary's authenticity, Hoff wrote:

> A great deal of evidence in support of child authorship can be found in a careful reading of the diary, for its detailed descriptions of events are such as could only have been recorded by someone seeing and experiencing them at the time. To a greater extent than might be explained by the unusual empathy of a twenty-year-old writer, they are given from the physical, mental, and emotional viewpoint of a child, telling what things were heavy, difficult to unfasten, too high to reach, hard to make sense of, frightening, irritating, or comforting. They reflect a child's nondifferentiation between what older people consider important or unimportant, and are communicated with

an intense, unselfconscious simplicity that no adult could have forged.

Hoff was also impressed by the fact that several scientists had analyzed the paper on which the diary was written. They agreed that it was manufactured before World War I—at least five years before its arrival in pieces in the office of *The Atlantic Monthly*.

Although Hoff accepted Opal's explanation of the origin of her diary, he did not swallow her claim to be the orphan of French nobility. He attributed that assertion to schizophrenia.

"It seems that from an early age, Opal had exhibited signs of what would now be known as schizophrenic behavior," he wrote in *The Singing Creek Where the Willows Grow*. "Opal's frequently strange conduct was apparently intensified by her tendency to eat poorly, deny herself food, or simply forget about meals—all of which she tended to do more and more as she grew older."

What became of Opal as she grew older—after her brief bout with literary fame? The story of her adult years is no less fantastic than that of her childhood.

A few years after Opal's move to England, Ellery Sedgwick learned that his young protegée had been spotted in India, where she was the guest of a wealthy maharajah. She had assumed the name Françoise Marie de Bourbon-Orléans and claimed to be "following in the footsteps" of her tiger-hunting father, Henri d'Orléans. For about five years, Opal lived at the Indian court, where her claim to be a French princess was taken seriously. She returned to Europe in 1926, spent two years living in an Austrian convent, then returned to England, where she studied briefly at Oxford. In 1948, authorities discovered her near starvation in Hampstead, living in a squalid little apartment crammed with books. She was committed to Napsbury Hospital, a mental institution near London where she lived until her death on February 17, 1992, at the age of ninety-four. To the end, those who knew her called her "Princess Françoise."

The mystery of Opal's identity will probably never be solved conclusively, but as Ellery Sedgwick insisted, the dubious story of her life should be judged separately from her lyrical legacy, *The Story of Opal.* After all, as Sedgwick pointed out:

> [T]he authorship does not matter, nor the life from which it came. There the book is. Nothing else is like it, nor apt to be. If there is alchemy in Nature, it is in children's hearts the unspoiled treasure lies, and for that room of the treasure house, *The Story of Opal* offers a tiny golden key. ⚜

BIBLIOGRAPHY

GENERAL REFERENCES

Blair, Karen J. *Women in Pacific Northwest History.* Seattle: University of Washington Press, 1988.

Carey, Charles Henry. *History of Oregon* (2 vols.). Chicago: The Pioneer Historical Publishing Co., 1922.

Corning, Howard McKinley, ed. *Dictionary of Oregon History.* Portland, OR: Binford & Mort, 1956.

Gaston, Joseph. *Centennial History of Oregon, 1811–1912.* Chicago: S. J. Clarke Publishing, 1912.

Gray, Dorothy. *Women of the West.* Millbrae, CA: Les Femmes, n.d.

James, Edward T., ed. *Notable American Women, 1607–1950* (3 vols.). Cambridge: Harvard University Press, 1971.

Leasher, Evelyn. *Oregon Women: A Bio-Bibliography.* Corvallis: Oregon State University Press, 1981.

Myres, Sandra L. *Westering Women and the Frontier Experience 1800–1915.* Albuquerque: University of New Mexico Press, 1982.

Reiter, Joan Swallow. *The Women.* Alexandria, VA: Time-Life Books, 1978.

Richey, Elinor. *Eminent Women of the West.* Berkeley, CA: Howell-North Books, 1975.

Smith, Helen Krebs, ed. *With Her Own Wings.* Portland, OR: Beattie & Co., 1948.

Ward, Jean M., and Maveety, Elaine A., eds. *Pacific Northwest Women 1815–1925.* Corvallis: Oregon State University Press, 1995.

BIBLIOGRAPHY

MARIE DORION

Barry, J. Neilson. "Madame Dorion of the Astorians," *The Oregon Historical Quarterly*, 1929.

Beckham, Cathy. "A Terrible Journey Had a Quiet Ending," *Capital Journal*, March 5, 1975.

Defenbach, Byron. *Red Heroines of the Northwest.* Caldwell, ID: The Caxton Printers, 1935.

Hunt, John Clark. "Woman of the Astorians," *Northwest Magazine*, January 4, 1970.

Irving, Washington. *Astoria.* Norman: University of Oklahoma Press, 1964. Originally published in 1836.

James, Carolyn (archivist for Oregon Department of Transportation). Letter to author, April 24, 1998.

Leipzig, Francis. "Madame Dorion Was Baptized, Buried at St. Louis Church," *Catholic Sentinel*, November 1, 1974.

"New Historic Marker to Be Dedicated." Press release from Oregon Travel Information Council, January 11, 1993.

Parkman, Frances. *The Oregon Trail.* New York: Signet Classic, 1950. Originally published in 1848.

Peltier, Jerome. *Madame Dorion.* Fairfield, WA: Ye Galleon Press, 1980.

Pogue, Anna Holm. "Madame Marie Dorion, Early Oregon Mother," in *With Her Own Wings*, ed. by Helen Krebs Smith. Portland, OR: Beattie & Co., 1948.

ANNA MARIA PITTMAN LEE

Allen, A. J. *Ten Years in Oregon: Travels and Adventures of Dr. E. White and Lady.* Ithaca, NY: 1848.

"Anna Maria," *Cascades: Magazine of Pacific Northwest Bell*, Winter 1965.

Brosnan, Cornelius J. *Jason Lee: Prophet of the New Oregon.* New York: The Macmillan Co., 1932.

Carey, Charles Henry. "Documentary: The Mission Record Book of the Methodist Episcopal Church," *Oregon History Quarterly*, September 1922.

Clark, Malcolm, Jr. *Eden Seekers: The Settlement of Oregon, 1818–1862.* Boston: Houghton-Mifflin Co., 1981.

Gay, Theressa. *The Life and Letters of Mrs. Jason Lee.* Portland, OR: Metropolitan Press, 1936.

Mattson, Sylvia. *Missionary Foot Paths: The Story of Anna Maria Pittman (Mrs. Jason Lee).* Salem, OR: Mission Mill Museum Association, 1978.

Nelson, Vera Joyce. "Anna Maria Pittman Lee," in *With Her Own Wings*, ed. by Helen Krebs Smith. Portland, OR: Beattie & Co., 1948.

TABITHA MOFFATT BROWN

Brown, Tabitha Moffatt. "Documents: A Brimfield Heroine—Mrs. Tabitha Brown," *The Quarterly of the Oregon Historical Society*, September 1904.

Easterling, Jerry. "Oregon's Pioneer Mother," *Statesman Journal*, May 7, 1987.

Ferrin, H. E. "Pacific University: Name of Mrs. Tabitha Brown, Plucky Woman of Early Days," *Oregon Sunday Journal*, November 14, 1909.

Goodman, Gloria Bledsoe. "Brown Left Her Mark," *Statesman Journal*, May 7, 1987.

Johnson, Jalmar. "Tabitha Brown—Small Package of Gumption," in *Builders of the Northwest.* New York: Dodd, Mead & Co., 1963.

Lockley, Fred. *Oregon Folks.* New York: The Knickerbocker Press, 1927.

Milliman, Loren. "Grandma Brown: Her Buckskin Needles Built a University," *Oregonian*, January 20, 1935.

———. "Grandma Brown: Concluding a Story of Great Pioneer Courage," *Oregonian*, January 27, 1935.

Reiter, Joan Swallow. *The Women.* Alexandria, VA: Time-Life Books, 1978.

BIBLIOGRAPHY

Sechrist, Steve (director of public affairs, Pacific University). Telephone interview, October 23, 1997, and letter to author, November 1997.

Smith, Jane Kinney. "Recollections of Grandma Brown," *The Quarterly of the Oregon Historical Society*, September 1902.

Spooner, Ella Brown. *Tabitha Brown's Western Adventures: A Grandmother's Account of Her Trek from Missouri to Oregon (1846–1858)*. New York: Exposition Press, 1958.

————. *The Brown Family History II.* Newton, KS: The Mennonite Press, 1929. Revised by Judith Young and Celista Platz, 1992.

Stewart, Eric. "The Birth of a University," *Library News*, Pacific University, (February 1997.) Originally published in *Old College Hall Messenger*, Fall 1990.

ABIGAIL SCOTT DUNIWAY

Duniway, Abigail Scott. "About Ourself," *The New Northwest*, May 5, 1871.

————. "A Few Recollections of a Busy Life," in *Souvenir of Western Women*, ed. by Mary Osborn Douthit. Portland, OR: Anderson & Duniway Co., 1905.

————. *Path Breaking: An Autobiographical History of the Equal Suffrage Movement in Pacific Coast States*. Portland, OR: James, Kerns & Abbott Co., 1914.

————. "Personal Reminiscences of a Pioneer," in *Portland, Oregon: Its History and Builders*, ed. by Joseph Gaston. Chicago: S. J. Clarke Publishing, 1911.

Duniway, David Cushing. "Abigail Scott Duniway, Path Breaker," in *With Her Own Wings*, ed. by Helen Krebs Smith. Portland, OR: Beattie & Co., 1948.

Johnson, Jalmar. *Builders of the Northwest*. New York: Dodd, Mead & Co., 1963.

Morrison, Dorothy Nafus. *Ladies Were Not Expected: Abigail Scott Duniway and Women's Rights*. Portland, OR: Oregon Historical Society Press, 1985. Originally published in 1977.

Moynihan, Ruth Barnes. "Of Women's Rights and Freedom: Abigail Scott Duniway," in *Women in Pacific Northwest History*, ed. by Karen J. Blair. Seattle: University of Washington Press, 1988.

————. *Rebel for Rights*. New Haven: Yale University Press, 1983.

Smith, Helen Krebs. *The Presumptuous Dreamers: A Sociological History of the Life and Times of Abigail Scott Duniway (1834–1915)*. Lake Oswego, OR: Smith, Smith & Smith Publishing Co., 1974.

BETHENIA OWENS-ADAIR

Dunlop, Richard. *Doctors of the American Frontier.* New York: Doubleday & Co., 1965.

Larsell, O. *The Doctor in Oregon: A Medical History.* Portland, OR: Binford & Mort, 1947.

Owens-Adair, Bethenia. *Dr. Owens-Adair: Some of Her Life Experiences.* Portland, OR: Mann & Beach Printers, 1906.

Walsh, Mary Roth. *Doctors Wanted: No Women Need Apply.* New Haven: Yale University Press, 1977.

MARY LEONARD

Aldrich, Myna. "Oregon's First Woman Lawyer," in *With Her Own Wings*, ed. by Helen Krebs Smith. Portland, OR: Beattie & Co., 1948.

Clark, Malcolm H., Jr. "The Lady and the Law: A Portrait of Mary Leonard," *Oregon Historical Quarterly*, June 1955.

Decker, Fred W. "Discovered: A Photo and More Facts about Mary Leonard, Oregon's First Woman Lawyer," *Oregon Historical Quarterly*, June 1977.

"A Woman Lawyer," *The Morning Oregonian*, April 15, 1886.

BIBLIOGRAPHY

LOLA GREENE BALDWIN

Bryant, Louise. "A Municipal Mother," *Sunset*, September 1912.

Hills, Tim. *The Many Lives of the Crystal Ballroom*. Gresham, OR: McMenamins Publishers & Brewery, 1997.

Myers, Gloria E. *A Municipal Mother: Portland's Lola Greene Baldwin, America's First Policewoman*. Corvallis: Oregon State University Press, 1995.

ALICE DAY PRATT

"Alice Day Pratt," in *The History of Crook County, Oregon*. Prineville: Crook County Historical Society, 1981.

Pratt, Alice Day. *A Homesteader's Portfolio*, with introduction by Molly Glass. Corvallis: Oregon State University Press, 1993. Originally published in 1922.

————. *Three Frontiers*. New York: Vantage Press, 1955.

Raban, Jonathan. *Bad Land: An American Romance*. New York: Pantheon, 1996.

HAZEL HALL

Bentley, Beth. "Beyond Walls and a Roof: The Hazel Hall-Harriet Monroe Correspondence," *Northwest Review*, 27, no. 3, 1989.

Curtis, Walt. "Hazel Hall: Northwest Poet," *Northwest Examiner*, December 1988.

Franklin, Viola Price. *A Tribute to Hazel Hall*. Caldwell, ID: The Caxton Printers, 1939.

"New Scholarship Will Enhance Hazel Hall's Legacy," *Heritage*, newsletter of the Oregon Cultural Heritage Commission, Summer 1997.

Parish, Phil. "Sweet Voice of Hazel Hall Is Hushed by Death," *Oregonian*, May 12, 1924.

Powers, Alfred. "Hazel Hall," in *History of Oregon Literature*. Portland, OR: Metropolitan Press, 1935.

Saul, George Brandon. "Wasted Flame? A Note on Hazel Hall and Her Poetry," in *Quintet: Essays on Five American Women Poets.* The Hague, Netherlands: Mouton & Co., 1967.

Staley, Darsee, and David Linder. "The Flowering of Hazel Hall," *Heritage,* newsletter of the Oregon Cultural Heritage Commission, Summer 1997.

Venn, George, ed. *From Here We Speak: An Anthology of Oregon Poetry.* Corvallis: Oregon State University Press, 1993.

OPAL WHITELEY

Bede, Elbert. *Fabulous Opal Whiteley.* Portland, OR: Binford & Mort, 1954.

Fortt, Inez. "Opal Whiteley: A Princess in Fairyland," *Old Oregon,* May–June 1969.

Hoff, Benjamin. *The Singing Creek Where the Willows Grow.* New York: Penguin Books, 1986.

Powers, Alfred. *History of Oregon Literature.* Portland, OR: Metropolitan Press, 1935.

Sedgwick, Ellery. *The Happy Profession.* Boston: Little, Brown & Co., 1946.

Whiteley, Opal. *Opal: The Journal of an Understanding Heart,* Adapted by Jane Boulton. New York: Crown Trade Paperbacks, 1984.

ℐNDEX

About the Author

Gayle C. Shirley launched the More Than Petticoats series in 1995 with her popular book on remarkable women from Montana history. She has written nine other books for Falcon Publishing, including *M is for Montana*, *Four-Legged Legends of Oregon*, and *Charlie's Trail: The Life and Art of C.M. Russell*.

Gayle wrote her first book, *Waddles*, the true story of a domestic goose, at the age of nine and has been writing, with varying degrees of commitment, ever since. She lives with her husband and two sons in Helena, Montana, where she finds it especially easy to indulge her passion for Western history.

More than Petticoats series

With in-depth and accurate coverage, this series pays tribute to the often unheralded efforts and achievements of the women who settled the West. Each title in the series includes a collection of absorbing biographies and b&w historical photos.

TWODOT
An Imprint of Falcon Publishing

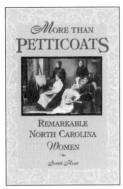

**More than Petticoats:
Remarkable North
Carolina Women**
by Scotti Kent
$12.95
ISBN 1-56044-900-4

**More than Petticoats:
Remarkable California
Women**
by Erin H. Turner
$9.95
ISBN 1-56044-859-8

**More than Petticoats:
Remarkable Montana
Women**
by Gayle C. Shirley
$8.95
ISBN 1-56044-363-4

**More than Petticoats:
Remarkable Oregon Women**
by Gayle C. Shirley
$9.95
ISBN 1-56044-668-4

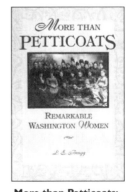

**More than Petticoats:
Remarkable Washington Women**
by L.E. Bragg
$9.95
ISBN 1-56044-667-6

TwoDot™ features books that celebrate and interpret the
rich culture and history of regional America.

To order check with your local bookseller or call Falcon® at **1-800-582-2665.**
*Ask for a FREE catalog featuring a complete list of titles on
nature, outdoor recreation, travel and regional history.*

FALCON®

www.falcon.com

Charles M. Russell

TWODOT®

The C. M. Russell Postcard Book
Co-published with the C. M. Russell Museum.

$8.95 sc
22 color postcards

Charles M. Russell, Legacy
By Larry Len Peterson
Co-published with the C. M. Russell Museum.

$95.00 cloth binding
456 pp

Charlie's Trail
The Life and Art of C. M. Russell
By Gayle C. Shirley
Co-published with the C. M. Russell Museum

$10.95 sc
72 pp

MONTANA HISTORICAL SOCIETY PRESS

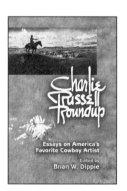

Charlie Russell Roundup
Essays on America's Favorite Cowboy Artist
Edited and with an introduction by Brian W. Dippie

$39.95 hc $19.95 sc
356 pp

Charlie Russell Journal

$12.95 hc
128 pp

To order, check with your local bookseller or call Falcon at **1-800-582-2665**.
Ask for a FREE catalog featuring a complete list of titles on nature, outdoor recreation, travel, and the West.

www.falcon.com

FALCON®